deported**dreams**deporte
eams**deported**dreams

Immigrant Youth and Families Resist Deportation

Edited by Kent Wong and Nancy Guarneros

Contributing editors: Angela Chuan-Ru Chen, Maurice Rafael Magaña, Julie Monroe, Gaspar Rivera-Salgado, Janna Shadduck-Hernández, and Ana K. Soltero López

UCLA Center for Labor Research and Education
Los Angeles, California

Cover photos courtesy of Samantha Sais.
Front: Renata Teodoro with her mother at the US-Mexico border.
Back: Renata Teodoro, Carlos Padilla, and Evelyn Rivera at the US-Mexico border.
Book design by Wendell Pascual.

UCLA Center for Labor Research and Education
Los Angeles, CA 90095-1478
© 2015 by UCLA Center for Labor Research and Education
All rights reserved. Published 2015
Printed in the United States of America

Library of Congress Control Number: 2015935022
ISBN 978-0-9836289-5-8

Dreams Deported tells the powerful, heart-wrenching stories of immigrant youth and their families who endure needless suffering at the hands of our government. This book illustrates the urgency of building a broad-based movement for basic human rights for all, a movement rooted in the recognition that every human being is worthy of care, compassion, and concern, no matter who you are, where you come from, or what you may have done. The time is long overdue to end not only mass incarceration but also mass deportation in America.

—Dr. Michelle Alexander, author of *The New Jim Crow: Mass Incarceration in the Age of Colorblindness*

Dreams Deported is the latest magnificent installment of what has turned into a modern-day *U.S.A.* trilogy. While the stories told here detail the heartbreak and devastation that occurs when families are torn apart by *la migra*, they also show the extraordinary drive and determination of undocumented youth making it in this country. These short, powerful vignettes will inspire and enrage and are must-reads for anyone who wants to understand the future of America.

—Gustavo Arellano, editor for *OC Weekly* and "¡Ask a Mexican!" columnist

Dreams Deported is a powerful book that lifts the stories of the undocumented immigrants who are facing the injustice of deportation. In the national debate on immigration, rarely are the voices of undocumented immigrants heard. *Dreams Deported* captures the stories of not only the deported but also the courageous immigrant youth and their families who are organizing for justice and human dignity.

—Pablo Alvarado, executive director of the National Day Laborer Organizing Network

Dreams Deported presents the powerful voices of young people who have experienced the trauma of deportation as well as their stories of resistance. My music video "Wake Me Up" features Hareth Andrade, one of the fearless immigrant youth featured in this book. Hareth represents a new generation of immigrant youth activists who are standing up, speaking out, and making change. This book captures the inspiring voices of the new immigrant youth movement.

—**Aloe Blacc,** Grammy-nominated recording artist

Dreams Deported conveys our immigrant experiences of inspiration, struggle, and resistance, using one of the most powerful tools of the immigrant youth movement: transformative, intimate storytelling. While US incarceration and deportation levels have hit world record highs and inflicted unspeakable pain on our families, a growing movement for justice has emerged from the shadows of fear and family separation. United We Dream thanks the UCLA Labor Center and all of this book's contributors for sharing the deep emotion and commitment we act on to keep our families together and create the world we want to live in. As this book illustrates and as Assata Shakur said, "We must love each other and support each other. We have nothing to lose but our chains."

—**Sofia Campos,** United We Dream

With vivid, compelling narratives that leap off the page, *Dreams Deported* reminds us what immigration has always been about: stories of courage, resilience, and hope—hope for our families and our future.

—**Jose Antonio Vargas,** award-winning journalist, filmmaker, and founder of Define American

What happens to a dream deferred?

Does it dry up
like a raisin in the sun?
Or fester like a sore—
And then run?
Does it stink like rotten meat?
Or crust and sugar over—
like a syrupy sweet?

Maybe it just sags
like a heavy load.

Or does it explode?

—Langston Hughes, "Harlem"

contents

Contents

foreword

This publication was produced by the students in a course I taught through the UCLA Center for Labor Research and Education in the 2013–2014 academic year. Teaching the class and working with the students was a remarkable experience. It was also a powerful personal journey and completed a circle that began many years ago.

Understanding the injustices undocumented immigrants face is something that I lived with for many years. I first learned I was undocumented while I was in high school. Although I had the grades and test scores to attend a four-year university, I was unable to afford it. Because of my immigration status, I was ineligible for federal financial aid or student loans. Instead, I attended Santa Monica City College as an AB 540 student (see Olivérez 2009, 7). After graduating from community college with an AA degree, I was able to transfer to UCLA.

I chose UCLA because it was close to home but mostly because I found a new home in the undocumented student organization IDEAS (Improving Dreams, Equality, Access and Success). I had the opportunity to attend an IDEAS banquet before I started at UCLA. The IDEAS students I met at the banquet were my heros. They proved that undocumented students like me could go to college and could succeed. I realized that this was the community I wanted to join. During that time, I was still trying to come to terms with my undocumented identity, as it had only been a year since I found out about my status. When I first learned about my undocumented status, I felt lonely

Nancy Guarneros lectures at UCLA, January 2015. *Courtesy of Alain Olavarrieta.*

and isolated. After the IDEAS banquet, I felt empowered.

I worked all summer and applied for various private scholarships to help pay for my first quarter at UCLA. I had only saved enough money for one quarter, but it was enough for me to get excited about attending UCLA. Eager to get started, I began browsing through the UCLA course web site.

One class caught my eye: Immigrant Rights, Labor, and Higher Education. My friends in IDEAS had mentioned this course as well. The focus of the course was on undocumented students in higher education. My first reaction was, "A class on *my* experience?"

The course instructors were Kent Wong and Victor Narro, two faculty members from the UCLA Labor Center. This was the first class in the country to focus on the experiences of undocumented students. The class had a different theme each week, integrated the latest research on immigration, and included an internship component that encouraged community engagement. For my internship, I worked with IDEAS to integrate what we were learning in class with practical outreach and education activities on campus. The students were able to learn about immigration history and policy while supporting the activities of IDEAS.

Of all my classes during my first quarter at UCLA, I enjoyed Kent and Victor's class the most. I felt empowered and like I belonged at UCLA. The course also provided an opportunity for me to give back, as it helped educate the UCLA community on the issues that mattered most to me.

In June 2009, I graduated from UCLA with a major in sociology and a minor in education. My dream of graduating from college became a reality with the support of my family, friends, and my IDEAS family. Graduation day marked a huge accomplishment in my life, but it was also a bittersweet day because I had to address my future plans. As an undocumented immigrant, I couldn't use the degree I had worked so hard for because I could not legally work. The federal DREAM Act, which would have provided undocumented students with a pathway to citizenship, was still being debated in Congress, and there was no progress on comprehensive immigration reform.

Through IDEAS, I met undocumented students who were attending graduate and professional schools, like Tam Tran at Brown University and Cinthya Felix at Columbia. Tam and Cinthya were both UCLA alumni and were well known among immigrant students nationally. They were pioneers, outspoken activists, and among the first undocumented students to attend graduate school. They gave hope to many of us who did not know what to do after college, and they paved the way for other undocumented students to pursue advanced degrees.

Since college was the only place I felt I had some freedom, I began the application process for a master's degree in education, in spite of the many barriers that still existed. I chose education for different reasons. First, I knew that in California, we were privileged to have AB 540, since most states did not have in-state tuition for undocumented students. During my graduate work, I wanted to learn more about the barriers to accessing higher education that many undocumented students encounter. Mostly, I wanted to contribute to the growing body of research about undocumented students. I believed there was a need for more scholars who could provide a firsthand undocumented perspective. Second, educators have always played an important role in my life. In some cases, they motivated me to stay in school when I wanted to give up. I dreamed of becoming a professor so I could motivate students myself one day.

I applied to colleges outside California even though I was concerned about how undocumented immigrants would be treated in other states. I wanted to see if I could get into these prestigious universities and if they would provide scholarships. To my surprise, I was accepted by many schools, including Harvard, Columbia, and Brown. But then I had to worry about funding my education. During the process of inquiring about financial aid, I learned that I had to educate many of the college admissions and financial aid representatives about undocumented students. Through many emails and phone calls, I would repeatedly explain, "Yes, I have lived in the United States my entire life; no, I do not have legal residency; and no, I am not an international student." For many of the campus representatives, this was the first time they had ever heard about undocumented students, and they did not know what to do. After extensive communications with the university staff, ultimately the answer was the same: "We would like to help, but we can't."

I narrowed my choices to two schools: UCLA or Harvard. At either university, I would have to pay for my education. After a lot of thought, I decided on UCLA. It seemed to be a better fit in terms of my academic work, but I also chose it because of my undocumented status. If I had gone to Harvard, I would have had to pay not only for tuition but also for travel, living expenses, and other costs that are associated with living away from home. I just didn't have the money. That decision-making process influenced my dissertation research on undocumented students' educational trajectories.

Just before starting the master's program at UCLA, I received more bad news. I had been awarded a private scholarship that would cover my tuition, but when the UCLA administration learned of my immigration status, they informed me that I was ineligible for the scholarship, and the money was withdrawn. In spite of this setback, I was determined to continue my education and began a new phase of my life as a master's student at UCLA. Although I was on the same campus, it felt like a different world. The amount of reading and writing was enormous, especially since I had to continue to work to support myself. And unlike the undergraduate program where I frequently had classes with friends from IDEAS, I was the only undocumented student in the entire graduate program.

During spring quarter 2010, Kent Wong asked me to be the teaching assistant for the Immigrant Rights, Labor, and Higher Education course, the same class I had taken during my first quarter at UCLA. Although I was excited to work on the class, my status continued to affect my access to opportunities enjoyed by my peers. Unlike other teaching assistants, I was ineligible for tuition remission because of my undocumented status.

We had sixty students enrolled in the class. I worked with a group of students to organize a campus forum to educate the UCLA community, including faculty and staff, about the issue of undocumented students. We planned the whole event, including creating the program, conducting outreach and mobilization, and managing logistics. Then right before the event took place, we heard the tragic news that our friends Tam Tran and Cinthya Felix had been killed in a car accident by a drunk driver. We were devastated.

Instead of a campus forum, the class prepared a memorial service at UCLA in honor of Tam and Cinthya. More than five hundred people attended, including Tam's and Cinthya's families and dozens of IDEAS alumni who returned to UCLA to honor their friends. All of the IDEAS alumni and current members gathered together on stage, embraced one another, and shared tears as we mourned the passing of our friends.

In fall 2010, the Immigrant Rights, Labor, and Higher Education class began work on a publication to honor the lives of Tam and Cinthya. The students in the class also began to collect stories from around the country chronicling the courageous acts of undocumented immigrant youth fighting for their rights. In 2012, the book *Undocumented and Unafraid: Tam Tran, Cinthya Felix, and the Immigrant Rights Movement* was published.

When I graduated from UCLA with a master's degree in education, I faced a dilemma once again. The federal DREAM Act had failed, and there had been no progress on immigration reform. Even with a master's degree, I still had no legal status and no opportunity to accept work where I could use my degrees.

My ultimate goal was to become a professor, so I knew I needed to obtain a PhD. I also knew that I wanted to contribute to the literature on undocumented students in higher education and that this would be the topic of my dissertation.

Although I was admitted to the UCLA PhD program in education, UCLA was unable to provide any financial aid because of my undocumented status. However, I was also admitted to Claremont Graduate University, a private university that provided me with a generous scholarship and faculty support. During my PhD program, I finally received permanent resident status and was granted work authorization. I had been waiting for this for more than twenty-five years and thought it would never happen. When it did, my life changed.

When I visited the UCLA Labor Center, I met with Kent Wong, shared the news about my work permit, and told him that I wanted to teach. He asked if I wanted to teach the Immigrant Rights, Labor, and Higher Education class at UCLA, the same class I had taken my first quarter at UCLA, the same class I had served as the teaching assistant for when I was in graduate school, and the same class that had organized the memorial for Tam and Cinthya. It made sense in every way for me to teach this course. I was getting my PhD in education, my dissertation was focused on undocumented students in higher education and for the first time, a former undocumented student would teach a course on undocumented students.

In the fall of 2013, I cotaught the class with Angela Chuan-Ru Chen and Ana K. Soltero López. The students participated in three main projects. Ana Soltero's team collected stories on the impact of deportations on our communities. Students interviewed undocumented youth who had faced the threat of deportation or who had family members who had faced deportation. These stories formed the foundation for this book. The students conducted preliminary interviews and presented final projects at the end of the class. During the winter and spring quarters of 2014, I taught the continuing courses with the students to develop this publication. Students conducted research, arranged and transcribed additional interviews, edited articles, and gathered photos and artwork. Kent Wong and I edited the stories to produce the third book in a series on immigrant youth published by the UCLA Labor Center.

I am proud of our students at UCLA who are carrying on the legacy of Tam Tran and Cinthya Felix and of IDEAS. I am grateful that I have been able to pursue my dream to teach and to conduct research on undocumented immigrant students. Finally, I hope that this publication will contribute to the advancement of the undocumented immigrant rights movement.

—Nancy Guarneros

Reference

Olivérez, Paz M., et al. 2009. "The College and Financial Aid Guide for: AB540 Undocumented Immigrant Students." The AB 540 College Access Network, Center for Higher Education Policy Analysis, University of Southern California. http://www.usc.edu/dept/chepa/pdf/AB%20540%20final.pdf.

preface

This publication began in a fall 2013 undergraduate course entitled Immigrant Rights, Labor, and Higher Education, offered by the UCLA Center for Labor Research and Education. The class was first offered in 2006, when the immigrant youth movement was just emerging. This book is the third in a series of student publications published by the UCLA Labor Center about the immigrant youth movement.

The first book, *Underground Undergrads: UCLA Undocumented Immigrant Students Speak Out*, was published in 2008. This breakthrough publication was the first of its kind written by and about undocumented immigrant students. The stories addressed the challenges and barriers facing undocumented immigrant youth and their daily struggle to survive and to pursue their college dreams. Because of concerns about the threat of deportation for the youth and their families, great care was taken to maintain their anonymity. The editors used pseudonyms, and the photographs concealed the identity of the students.

The second book, *Undocumented and Unafraid: Tam Tran, Cinthya Felix, and the Immigrant Youth Movement*, was published in 2012. The book was a tribute to two UCLA undocumented student alumni who were tragically killed by a drunk driver in 2010. Courageous leaders of the immigrant youth movement, scholars, and activists, Tam's and Cinthya's lives epitomized the struggle of immigrant youth. The second publication also captured stories of the emerging national immigrant youth movement, especially the fierce,

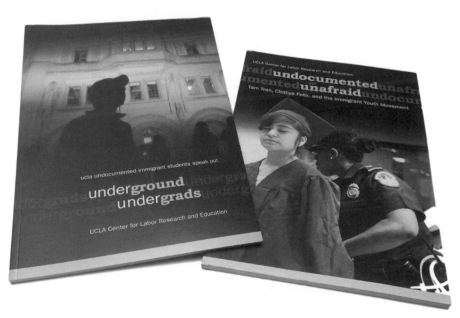

Courtesy of Wendell Pascual.

powerful campaigns in 2010 to support passage of the federal DREAM Act, which would have provided a pathway to citizenship for undocumented youth. *Undocumented and Unafraid* used real names, exhibited bold photographs, and featured the voices of a new movement of undocumented youth who refused to remain in the shadows.

This book, *Dreams Deported: Immigrant Youth and Families Resist Deportation*, is the third written and edited by UCLA students, many of whom are immigrants or from immigrant families. Immigrant youth have emerged as outspoken leaders of the immigration reform movement. They have expanded their campaign to include the fight for all immigrants and to oppose the policies of deportation that have criminalized their communities. Part One captures stories of the deported, focusing on the impact on family and community. Part Two features stories of resistance to deportation. The final section is a resource guide with information on deportation and ways to become involved in the human rights movement.

The UCLA Labor Center is proud of this book and the other two publications in the series, which have helped to lift the voices of undocumented youth and have supported a growing immigrant youth movement. Immigrant youth represent the hope and future of immigrant communities. These young people have emerged from the shadows, found the power of their voices, built national networks, and demonstrated tremendous commitment and courage in their pursuit of civil and human rights. They have established themselves as the moral authority on the front lines of the immigration debate and have expanded their campaign far beyond their own self-interest, to embrace all immigrants and our society as a whole.

The debate on deportation and immigration policy continues in Congress, in the state legislatures, in our communities, and in our classrooms. It is our hope that this book will contribute to a deeper understanding of the human impact of deportations and inspire more immigrant youth to pursue social and economic justice.

Immigrant Rights, Labor, and Higher Education class, October 2013. *Courtesy of Liana Ghica.*

acknowledgments

We are deeply appreciative of the UCLA students from the 2013 Immigrant Rights, Labor, and Higher Education class who dedicated many hours to interview, transcribe, and edit the stories featured in this book: Arturo Aguirre, Blanca Alcántara, Jessica Álvarez, Ludimila Alves, Shealy Blanco, Abigail Cabrera, Brenda Camarillo, Kryssia Campos, Magdalena Ceja, Karina Cervantes, Zitao Chen, Miriam Contreras, Marlette Cortez, Kyle Cowen, Jonathan Cruz-Carrera, Karla Dávalos, María Delgado, Dinah Domínguez, María J. Duque, Gerleroz Exconde, Christian Frial, Stephanie García, Brianne Guerra, María Gutiérrez, Yadira Hernández, Diana Lonescu, Sofía Jácome, Mayra Jones, Zara Khachatryan, Jacqueline Kim, Pik Lee, Li Linfeng, Yu Hui-Lin (Amy Lin), Yessenia Macías, Christopher Mandalian, Larissa Martínez, Tania Mendoza, Anabel Meza, Grecia Mondragón, María Moreno-Oseguera, Cristina Mosqueda, Anais Muñoz, Angélica Muñoz, Berenice Muñoz, Aryan Nikki Narvasa, Denise Panaligan, Harvey Peralta, Andrea Pérez, Velen Pérez, Karina Pérez, Mario Pizarro, Valerie Quirate, Erika Ramírez, Reuben Ronquillo, Christopher Rosas, Antonette Sadile, Miguel Sánchez, Roció Trujillo, Mía Vasquez-Gutierrez, Susana Vázquez, Crystal Villalpando, and Francis Villaruz. Angela Chuan-Ru Chen and Ana K. Soltero López were part of the teaching team.

It is not easy to share these stories of pain and separation that have deeply impacted the lives of immigrants. We are grateful for the people who were willing to share their stories with us: Yves Gomes, Adrian González, Steve Li, the Bravo family, Renata Teodoro, Ju Hong, Luis Leon, Ilse Escobar, Hareth Andrade, Cristina Ramirez, Edgar Akopyan, Erika Andiola, and members of the National Immigrant Youth Alliance and United We Dream.

We also thank those who helped collect photos and artwork, especially María Duque, as well as the photographers and artists who allowed us to share their work: Samantha Sais, Blue Gutiérrez, Osvaldo Fortes, Adrian González, Steve Pavey, Faviana Rodríguez, Raymundo Hernández, Liana Ghica, Alain Olavarrieta, IDEAS at UCLA, Seth Ronquillo, Serouj Ourishian, Datev Arman, James Oakfield, The California Endowment, Pocho1, Aloe Blacc, and the National Immigrant Youth Alliance. We also appreciate Abel Valenzuela, Victor Narro, and Mario De Leon for their support for the project.

A special thank you to Wendell Pascual for the beautiful book design and to dedicated immigration attorneys Angelo Mathay and Malou Chavez for their review of the introduction and resource section. Finally, we want to thank the staff of the UCLA Labor Center and the Dream Resource Center for their continuous support in advancing the rights of immigrants in this country.

introduction

Background on the Immigrant Youth Movement

The undocumented immigrant youth movement has emerged as a powerful force throughout the country, especially in California, which is home to the largest population of undocumented youth (Immigration Policy Center 2012, 2). In 2001, California Assembly Bill 540 (AB 540) provided the opportunity for undocumented students to attend college without having to pay exorbitant out-of-state tuition. This legislative change opened the door for a new generation of undocumented youth to enter higher education. Undocumented youth began organizing on college campuses, creating student groups to support immigrant youth access to and retention in higher education, and providing resources to other undocumented college students across the nation.

The immigrant youth movement was instrumental in the 2011 passage of the California Dream Act, Assembly Bills 130 and 131, which allowed undocumented immigrants access to state financial aid. Undocumented youth were also active in other recent California legislative victories, such as driver's license implementation for undocumented immigrants, the TRUST Act, which bars local law enforcement from colluding with immigration enforcement, and health care access for Deferred Action for Childhood Arrivals grantees, including Medi-Cal and other state-funded programs for low-income individuals.

The national campaign for the 2010 federal DREAM Act, which would have provided a path to citizenship for undocumented youth, led to the growth of a nationwide immigrant youth movement. Although the federal DREAM Act failed to pass the Senate in December 2010, immigrant youth continued to emerge from the shadows and develop innovative organizing techniques to campaign for the rights of all 11 million undocumented immigrants in this country. A central demand from campaigns led by immigrant youth has been to stop deportations, which have criminalized immigrant communities, torn apart families, and led to immense suffering among undocumented immigrants.

In spite of his 2008 campaign pledge to enact immigration reform, President Obama has been responsible for the largest mass deportation in the country's history, deporting more than 2 million people from 2009 to 2014 (Lopez 2011, 3). The Obama administration expanded the Secure Communities program, which aggressively encouraged local law enforcement agencies to collaborate with Immigration and Customs Enforcement and effectively stripped many immigrants of legal protections. Due to the increased threat of deportation, many victims of crimes are afraid to call the police.

In 2010, the undocumented immigrant youth movement launched the "Education Not Deportation" campaign to stop the deportation of undocumented immigrant youth. The campaign secured dozens of victories, stopping the deportation of immigrant youth, one after another. But individual campaigns were not enough to stem the systematic detention and deportation of immigrant youth and their families.

Following the failure of the DREAM Act in Congress, immigrant youth groups launched the "Right to Dream" campaign in 2011 to demand that the Obama administration stop the deportation of undocumented immigrant youth. Campaign leaders met with the White House staff and pressured President Obama to use his executive power. During the 2012 presidential election season, activists held sit-ins at several Obama for America reelection campaign offices in battleground states, demanding that Obama take action.

The immigrant youth movement scored a huge victory in June 2012 when President Obama announced Deferred Action for Childhood Arrivals (DACA), the first major immigration policy breakthrough in over twenty-five years. DACA provided undocumented youth with a two-year reprieve from the threat of deportation and the opportunity to apply for work permits. DACA was designed as a temporary fix to provide relief to immigrant youth age sixteen to thirty and to encourage the passage of comprehensive immigration reform. More than six hundred thousand immigrant youth applied for DACA by 2014 (Singer 2013).

In 2013, a comprehensive immigration reform bill called the Border Security, Economic Opportunity, and Immigration Modernization Act (S.744), passed the Senate but failed in the House of Representatives. While S.744 called for legalization and a path to citizenship for undocumented immigrants, it also included militarization of the border and harsh enforcement policies, measures opposed by undocumented youth. Congressional debate on immigration has continued to no avail, with both political parties failing to enact comprehensive immigration reform.

While Congress stalled, immigrant youth began to advocate for the expansion of DACA for all 11 million undocumented immigrants. In August 2014, President Obama claimed he would consider expanding DACA to include more people but in concession to political pressures related to the midterm elections, he failed to act.

The deportation industry continues to grow in this country, extracting profits from the suffering of immigrant communities. In 2011, the Department of Homeland Security held a record-breaking 429,000 immigrants in over 250 facilities across the country and currently maintains a daily capacity of 33,400 beds (American Civil Liberties Union 2014). Deportation centers are notorious for their inhumane conditions, including overcrowded quarters, extreme temperatures, poor and insufficient food, and glaring lights twenty-four hours a day.

Immigrant youth have courageously organized sit-ins and chained themselves to the front of Immigration and Customs Enforcement detention centers to physically stop buses from deporting families and children. Other undocumented activists have infiltrated detention centers to gather information from detainees that challenged the administration claims that "low-priority" immigrants were not being targeted for deportation. Activists recorded inmate stories that were used to expose abusive conditions and launch campaigns to free immigrants who were unjustly held.

In the summer of 2013, undocumented youth organized the "Bring Them Home" campaign to draw attention to immigrant youth who had lived many years in this country but had been deported or had voluntarily left. For the first time in history, a group of undocumented students successfully challenged immigration policy by leading a national campaign to return to the United States after being deported or leaving the country voluntarily.

Frequently Asked Questions on Immigration, Detention, and Deportation

Who is undocumented?

"Undocumented" is an informal term to describe anyone who is not a US citizen or legal permanent resident and who has no government authorization to be in the United States. The immigrant rights community prefers the term "undocumented" over "illegal" or "illegal alien," which are considered pejorative and dehumanizing.

Undocumented status applies to people who enter the country without permission but can also apply to those who initially entered with permission, for example, those whose tourist or student visas have expired or whose request for entry or asylum is denied.

There are approximately 11 million undocumented people living in the United States. According to the Pew Hispanic Center, 57 percent of undocumented immigrants are from Mexico, 23 percent from other Latin American countries, 10 percent from Asia, 5 percent from Europe and Canada, and 5 percent from other areas (Passel 2011, 10).

What is deportation, and who can be deported?

According to US Citizenship and Immigration Services, deportation is "the formal removal of an undocumented person from the United States, through either the issuance of a formal removal order or a more informal removal process." Any noncitizen can be deported, including legal permanent residents; refugees; people who have been granted asylum, "withholding of removal," or "temporary protected status;" those in the process of adjusting status; and those on student, business, or other visas (National Immigration Law Center 2002).

Who is considered low priority and high priority for deportation?

The Department of Homeland Security (DHS) and Immigration and Customs Enforcement (ICE) have issued guidelines to determine who is considered low priority and high priority. Some of the factors that determine priority status include: length of residence in the United States, age, armed forces membership, education level (high school, college, or advanced degree) in the United States, marriage to a US citizen or a legal permanent resident, children who are US citizens, and criminal history. According to DHS, there are three categories of noncitizens who should be considered priorities for deportation: those with criminal histories, with a history of "egregious" immigration violations, and who recently crossed the border. *Recent* is usually defined as within the last three years (Canizales 2014, 11).

Send 'Em Home

Approximate number of deportations by fiscal year, 1981-2013*

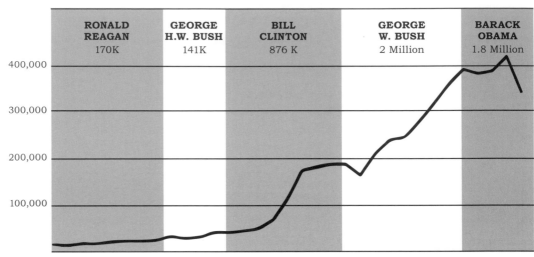

*Includes official removals only, 2013 numbers through September 7, 2013
Source: Department of Homeland Security

Source: AJ Vicens, "The Obama Administration's 2 Million Deportations, Explained," *Mother Jones*, April 4, 2014, http://www
.motherjones.com/politics/2014/04/obama-administration-record-deportations.

Fiscal Year 2014 ICE Immigration Removals:

The leading countries of origin for removals were Mexico, Guatemala, Honduras, and
El Salvador.

315,943

Removals conducted by ICE

102,224

Individuals apprehended in
the interior of the United States

213,719

Individuals apprehended while
attempting to unlawfully enter
the United States

177,960

Individuals who were previously
convicted of a crime

2,802

Classified as suspected or
confirmed gang members

137,983

Individuals removed who
had no criminal conviction

Source: U.S. Immigration and Customs Enforcement, http://www.ice.gov/removal-statistics.

Who controls deportations?

The US system of detention and deportation is shaped by policies, legislation, and case law. ICE oversees the detention and deportation process. Specifically, ICE's Office of Detention and Removal is in charge of identifying, detaining, and deporting noncitizens in the United States. Through the congressional appropriations process, Congress influences ICE (including Customs and Border Protection and other enforcement agencies) by allocating funding to hire border patrol agents and detention center staff. Congress has also set quotas for the agency to detain and deport four hundred thousand immigrants per year (US Department of Homeland Security 2013). Since 2008, immigration detention facilities have held an average of thirty thousand detainees per day. Under the Obama administration, more than 2 million people have been deported (Fitz 2013).

What policies have resulted in the increase of deportations?

Secure Communities is the key program that has facilitated mass deportations. Secure Communities is a nationwide program that was launched by former DHS Secretary Michael Chertoff and expanded under former DHS Secretary Janet Napolitano. This program promotes collaboration between local law enforcement and ICE. When an individual is detained or arrested, fingerprint records are cross checked against the databases of all law enforcement agencies to identify both criminal history and immigration status.

Secure Communities has greatly increased the detention and deportation of nonviolent immigrants who do not pose a threat to public safety, do not have criminal histories, and are not repeat immigration offenders. Many detainees and deportees have been apprehended for minor traffic violations, such as driving without a license, or immigration-related offenses (Detention Watch Network 2010, 23).

Data maintained by ICE revealed that from the program's inception in 2008 until June 2010, 79 percent of the people deported under Secure Communities were "non-criminals or were picked up for lower level offenses." According to this same data released by ICE, "only 21% were charged with or convicted of a serious felony" (American Civil Liberties Union 2010).

Secure Communities has undermined trust between immigrant communities and local police departments, thereby threatening public safety by making immigrants less likely to contact the police when they are victims or witnesses of crimes.

What is the status of comprehensive immigration reform (CIR) legislation in Congress?

For many years, there has been fierce debate in Congress regarding comprehensive immigration reform. Certain bills such as S.744 have included increased border security and punitive restrictions on existing immigrants and future immigration, along with provisions to legalize the status of some undocumented immigrants. The punitive measures have included long waiting periods for immigrants to apply for legal status, fines for violating immigration laws, varying requirements that would make many undocumented immigrants ineligible for legalized status, and "guest worker" provisions that would establish temporary work visas for immigrants with no pathway to permanent legal residency.

Debate has also focused on whether undocumented immigrants should be provided with a path to citizenship. Fearing for their political future, many Republican congressional representatives have opposed legalization of undocumented immigrants. The vast majority of immigrants are people of color who have historically voted in higher numbers for Democrats.

Congress enacted the last major immigration reform in 1986, and there is currently no consensus on an approach to comprehensive immigration reform.

Can President Obama stop deportations?

The president has administrative authority to enforce immigration policies that could dramatically impact deportations. The administration could eliminate the Secure Communities program and sever the collaboration between local law enforcement agencies and ICE. And President Obama could end the deportation quota (Narro 2013).

In June of 2012, Obama provided administrative relief for undocumented youth through DACA. DACA grants temporary protection from deportation and a two-year work permit to qualified undocumented youth. This policy has impacted the lives of more than six hundred thousand undocumented youth (Singer 2013).

In November 2014, Obama expanded DACA with a broader initiative called Deferred Action for Parents of Americans (DAPA). DAPA defers deportation for some undocumented parents whose children are citizens or permanent residents. According to DHS, up to 4.4 million people may qualify for DAPA (US Citizenship and Immigration Services 2014).

Who is impacted by deportations?

Deportations do not just impact undocumented immigrants. Legal permanent residents and US citizens are also directly affected by deportations. Many immigrant families are "mixed-status" families. For instance, many children of undocumented immigrants are US citizens who have never lived in another country. Among the children in a single family, one could be a US citizen, one protected under DACA, and another undocumented. There are approximately 4.5 million children who are US citizens with at least one undocumented parent (Taylor 2011, 6). And those children are losing their parents: "In the last 10 years, over 100,000 immigrant parents of U.S. children have been deported from the U.S." (Chaudry 2010, 15).

How have undocumented youth stopped deportations?

Undocumented youth across the county have come out of the shadows and embraced the slogan "Undocumented and Unafraid." By sharing their stories publicly, they have changed the image of what it means to undocumented. National networks of undocumented youth have organized rallies, protests, and civil disobedience actions to stop deportations across the nation, using social media as a tool to mobilize people, circulate online petitions, and generate public awareness.

References

American Civil Liberties Union. 2010. "ACLU Statement on Secure Communities." November 10. https://www.aclu.org/immigrants-rights/aclu-statement-secure-communities.

American Civil Liberties Union. 2014. "Immigration Detention." https://www.aclu.org/immigrants-rights/immigration-detention.

Canizales, Carolina, et al. 2014. "Deportation Defense: A Guide for Members of Congress and Other Elected Officials." United We Dream. http://unitedwedream.org/wp-content/uploads/2014/06/DeportationDefenseGuide_2014_print.pdf.

Chaudry, Ajay, et al. 2010. "Facing Our Future: Children in the Aftermath of Immigration Enforcement." The Urban Institute. February. http://www.urban.org/UploadedPDF/412020_FacingOurFuture_final.pdf.

Detention Watch Network. 2010. "Deportation 101: A Community Resource on Anti-Deportation Education and Organizing." May. http://www.nationalimmigrationproject.org/Deportation101_LowRes_January_2011.pdf.

Fitz, Marshall. 2013. "The Immigration Enforcement Paradox." Center for American Progress. January 4. http://www.americanprogress.org/issues/immigration/news/2013/01/04/48968/the-immigration-enforcement-paradox/.

Immigration Policy Center. 2012. "Who and Where the DREAMers Are, Revised Estimates." American Immigration Council. October. http://www.immigrationpolicy.org/sites/default/files/docs/who_and_where_the_dreamers_are_two.pdf.

Lopez, Mark Hugo, Ana Gonzalez-Barrera, and Seth Motel. 2011. "As Deportations Rise to Record Levels, Most Latinos Oppose Obama's Policy: President's Approval Rating Drops, but Obama Has a Big Lead over 2012 GOP Rivals." Pew Hispanic Center, Pew Research Center. December 28. http://www.pewhispanic.org/files/2011/12/Deportations-and-Latinos.pdf.

Narro, Victor. 2013. "The President Can Fix the Broken Immigration System Today." *The Blog*, *The Huffington Post*. October 21. http://www.huffingtonpost.com/victor-narro/the-president-can-fix-the_b_4134011.html.

National Immigration Law Center. 2002. "Guide to Immigrant Eligibility for Federal Programs." 4th ed. http://www.nilc.org/guidefed.html.

Passel, Jeffrey S., and D'Vera Cohn. 2011. "Unauthorized Immigrant Population: National and State Trends." Pew Hispanic Center, Pew Research Center. http://www.pewhispanic.org/files/reports/133.pdf.

Singer, Audrey, and Nicole Prchal Svajlenka. 2013. "Immigration Facts: Deferred Action for Childhood Arrivals (DACA)." Brookings Metropolitan Policy Program. August 14. http://www.brookings.edu/~/media/research/files/reports/2013/08/14-daca/daca_singer_svajlenka_final.pdf.

Taylor, Paul, et al. 2011. "Unauthorized Immigrants: Length of Residency, Patterns of Parenthood." Pew Hispanic Center, Pew Research Center. December 1. http://www.pewhispanic.org/files/2011/12/Unauthorized-Characteristics.pdf.

US Department of Homeland Security. 2013. "FY 2013 ICE Immigration Removals." https://www.ice.gov/removal-statistics-2013.

US Citizenship and Immigration Services. 2014. "Executive Actions on Immigration." http://www.uscis.gov/immigrationaction#2.

Part I

stories of deportation

Top: Adrian González and his siblings reunite with their parents at the US-Mexico border, June 2014.
Bottom: The González family at the US-Mexico border, June 2014. *Both photos courtesy of Blu Gutierrez.*

Adrian González and his mother at the US-Mexico border, June 2014. *Courtesy of Blu Gutierrez.*

Undocumented immigrant families have long suffered from living in the shadows under the constant threat of deportation. During the first six years of the Obama administration, there were more than 2 million deportations (Lopez 2011, 3). The massive increase in deportations is the result of stepped-up community and workplace raids by ICE and increased collaboration between local law enforcement and federal immigration agents. Consequently, undocumented immigrants fear law enforcement to the point that many crime victims do not notify the police, resulting in increased crime levels and leaving undocumented immigrants even more vulnerable.

The most immediate impact of deportation is the devastating separation of immigrant families. Every day when undocumented mothers and fathers go to work, they worry that they may be detained, deported, and separated from their children. Mixed-status families, with some documented and some undocumented members, also live under the constant fear of being separated. Deportations not only devastate the lives of the deported, they also punish those who are left behind. Deportation of undocumented parents causes trauma among their children, who are sent to live with relatives or forced to fend for themselves. This ongoing, daily reality for immigrant communities is seldom covered in the mainstream news. And all the while, Congress debates immigration policy month after month, year after year, while refusing to take action.

The financial cost of deportation is immeasurable for immigrant families, who are already among the poorest and most economically vulnerable within our society. When parents are deported and can no longer work to support their families, the economic impact is devastating. Families are left destitute, some face eviction, and family members who remain must work even longer hours than before to survive. The cumulative impact on immigrant communities is also overwhelming: more families in overcrowded housing, more homelessness, greater poverty, and more children facing hunger and deprivation.

Deportations are more than just statistics. The victims of deportation are neighbors and members of our community, and how we treat them defines who we are as a society.

This section shares the stories of undocumented families and the impact deportation has on immigrant communities. These stories capture the human dimension of deportations that rarely receives attention from the media, from the government agencies that implement deportations, or from elected officials who have failed to address the crisis of immigration reform.

Reference

Lopez, Mark Hugo, Ana Gonzalez-Barrera, and Seth Motel. 2011. "As Deportations Rise to Record Levels, Most Latinos Oppose Obama's Policy: President's Approval Rating Drops, but Obama Has a Big Lead over 2012 GOP Rivals." Pew Hispanic Center, Pew Research Center. December 28. http://www.pewhispanic.org/files/2011/12/Deportations-and-Latinos.pdf.

At first, **Carlos did not
want his children**
to come to the **detention center**;
he could **not bear the thought**
of his children
seeing him behind bars,
locked up like a **criminal**.

father of ucla student deported

Yessenia Macias

The names in the story are pseudonyms

Cristina Ramirez graduated from the University of California, Los Angeles, in 2013 with a degree in psychology. She is studious, ambitious, and determined. Although she is a US citizen, her father is undocumented, and he was deported while she was enrolled at UCLA. Her father's deportation turned her life upside down and to this day, her family has not recovered from the trauma, either emotionally or financially.

Cristina's parents, Carlos and Lupe, grew up in Jalisco, Mexico. They fell in love and had dreams of having a family and owning a home. But they knew that economic opportunities in Mexico were very limited. Together, they decided they would migrate to the United States to pursue their dreams.

Carlos tried to cross the border first. It took several attempts before he was successful. He first tried walking through the desert. Later he hid in boxes in truck beds, but he was apprehended and sent back each time. Finally, he crossed through the Arizona desert and then hid in a car until he arrived at a safe place.

A year later, Carlos helped Lupe come to the United States. Carlos was the first one in his family to come to the United States, so he did not have the support of a family network. Carlos and Lupe immediately began looking for work. Carlos was able to find work in the construction industry. Lupe provided child care for other families. Things were going well for Carlos and Lupe. They had work, and they were able to pay for food and shelter.

Three years after coming to the United States, Carlos and Lupe had their first child, a beautiful baby girl they named Cristina. Four years later, Maria was

UCLA students against deportation. *Courtesy of IDEAS at UCLA.*

born. Both of their children were born in the United States and were therefore US citizens.

One of the biggest obstacles Carlos faced was the language barrier. Cristina recalls when she was a young girl, watching how frustrated and stressed her father was when he couldn't communicate with English-speaking people. One day, Carlos wanted to pick up dinner for Cristina since her mother was running late at work. At the fast food restaurant, the cashier kept saying, "I don't understand you, sir." Instead of giving up, he went to the next fast food restaurant and tried ordering again, this time successfully.

Carlos was a proud family man. He was the primary breadwinner who worked hard, paid the bills, and provided for his family. Carlos always spoke Spanish at home. He wanted his children to learn their native language as a connection to their culture and to their family back in Mexico.

After Maria was born, Carlos and Lupe decided to buy their first home. They consulted a realtor and discovered that because of their undocumented status, they were restricted from obtaining loans and signing the legal documents. Although

they were frustrated and worried, Carlos and Lupe kept trying. They found a friend who had a social security number who was willing to purchase the home in his name, while Carlos paid all the expenses. They moved to Orange County, California, to a city with a large Mexican immigrant community that they grew to love. Soon, there were two more additions to the family, Carlitos and Eric.

From the time she was a young girl, Cristina's family emphasized education. They instilled in her the belief that going to college would open doors. In high school, Cristina excelled academically, enrolled in advanced placement classes, and engaged in extracurricular activities that would help her gain admittance to college.

Cristina was thrilled when she was admitted to UCLA, her dream school. During her senior year in high school, she attended a UCLA tour for prospective students and fell in love with the campus. She had never seen such a beautiful school. The location was also perfect for Cristina; the distance provided her independence but was close enough for her to go home regularly.

UCLA student rally, May 2014. *Courtesy of Seth Ronquillo.*

When **graduation day finally arrived**, it was bittersweet. Cristina cried because she knew **she could not share this moment with her father**.

Because of the long commute from Orange County to UCLA, Cristina found a part-time job so she could afford to live near campus. On weekends, Cristina went home to visit her family. She loved spending time with her siblings. They were her motivation to do well in school, and she wanted to encourage them to excel in school and attend college.

Everything was going well for the Martinez family until the economic recession hit. As a construction worker, Carlos felt the impact deeply. There were fewer and fewer construction jobs, and the family suffered financially. Although Cristina's mom worked as a caregiver, it was not enough to cover their monthly expenses. Carlos was desperate to continue providing for his family, so he opened a small business and set up a mobile car wash.

One night, Cristina and her family were awakened by a phone call. Cristina picked up the phone and heard an operator say, "Will you accept the charges?" Cristina knew that the news she was going to hear was not good. Her father had been in a car accident and because he was undocumented and did not have a license, they towed his car. Two weeks later, Carlos was pulled over again. This time instead of issuing a ticket, the officer checked Carlos's record, saw the prior accident, and arrested him. The officer also conducted an immigration check and referred the case to immigration agents who placed Carlos in deportation proceedings. In Orange County, police frequently turn over suspected undocumented immigrants to immigration authorities. This policy was the result of the Secure Communities program implemented by the Department of Homeland Security in 2008, which requires local law enforcement agencies to turn over suspected undocumented immigrants to Immigration and Customs Enforcement for deportation.

At first, Carlos did not want his children to come to the detention center; he could not bear the thought of his children seeing him behind bars, locked up like a criminal. But Cristina's youngest brother, Eric, cried and cried every day and asked questions about where his father went and why he was not coming home. Lupe finally decided that they should all go to visit her husband. She was worried that this might be the last time her children would see their father.

Carlos was held in the detention center for three months before he was deported to Mexico. Those three months were the most difficult time for Cristina and her family. They were forced to move out of their home because they could no longer afford the mortgage payments. They began renting a room from a family in the area. Lupe and her four children shared a single room until they were able to find a place they could afford. As the oldest, Cristina felt the responsibility to contribute financially to help her family. She found a second job in an accounting firm in order to supplement her mother's income. Cristina's sister was seventeen years old when her father was deported and although she was still in high school, she also got a job to help support the family.

Cristina tried to seek legal help. When she was not in school or at work, she spent her time on the phone seeking advice from attorneys to help her father. But no one was able to stop her father's deportation.

The deportation proceedings not only impacted Cristina emotionally and financially but also took a toll on her studies. She tried to manage school, full-time work, and helping take care of her younger siblings. But it was difficult to concentrate on her schoolwork, knowing that her father was in a detention center. Cristina feared she would fall into depression, so she sought counseling on campus. She also relied on the support of her close friends and family.

During this same period, UCLA announced that Janet Napolitano, the former director of the Department of Homeland Security who oversaw Immigration and Customs Enforcement, would become the new president of the University of California system. Cristina remembers being filled with fear, knowing that Napolitano was responsible for deporting so many immigrants. Although a US citizen herself, Cristina was scared that the UC president might harm immigrant students and their families.

Cristina persevered through the tears and sleepless nights. When graduation day finally arrived, it was bittersweet. Cristina cried because she knew she could not share this moment with her father. Carlos had

UCLA students at immigration action, July 2013. *Courtesy of IDEAS at UCLA.*

IDEAS table at a youth conference, November 2014. *Courtesy of IDEAS at UCLA.*

crossed the border in search of his dreams and made countless sacrifices for his family, but he was not able to see his daughter walk the stage at UCLA.

After Carlos was deported, Cristina's mother and siblings were able to contact him by phone through her aunt and grand-mother back in Mexico. Cristina's family was now in two different countries with no immediate hope of being reunited. Her mother has expressed thoughts of moving back to Mexico to be with her husband, but she stays in the United States because she wants a better education for Cristina's

younger brothers. Cristina makes an extra effort to share happy memories about her father with her siblings, especially because she fears that her youngest brother will forget who his father was.

After graduating from UCLA, Cristina moved to the East Coast and joined the Teach for America program. She is currently teaching Spanish in a public school. Her sister will begin college next year. Cristina continues to stay in close touch with her family. She goes home for the holidays and talks on the phone with her dad, who is still in Mexico.

Grant High School had a large
Armenian community,
so Edgar was able to
quickly make friends
and find his way around.
These high-school friends soon
became his family
in the United States.

through a glass window

Zara Khachatryan
The names in the story are pseudonyms

Edgar Akopyan was born and raised in Yerevan, Armenia. At the age of fifteen, he was given the opportunity to travel to the United States to perform with his martial arts group for several months. Edgar knew that the opportunity to go to the United States was extraordinary. He had heard that America was the "land of the free," a place where there were endless opportunities to become successful. In Armenia, higher education was limited to a few, wealthy families.

During the thirteen-hour flight from Armenia to the United States, he contemplated how this trip could potentially lead to a permanent move. At the same time, he was also thinking about how he would miss his family, his friends, and his hometown.

Edgar arrived in North Hollywood, California, on July 3, 1997, and moved into a one-bedroom apartment with his grandmother. For about three months, he participated in weekly competitions all over California. Time was flying by, and he was still trying to get used to the fast-paced schedule and to the American lifestyle. After his visa expired, he became undocumented. Many Armenians who visit the United States on a tourist visa have been able to regularize their status through political asylum, by proving that they would be subject to political or religious persecution in

Edgar's hometown of Yerevan, Armenia. *Courtesy of Serouj Ourishian.*

Armenia. But Edgar did not have access to legal counsel or advice.

The biggest challenge Edgar faced was the language barrier. In September, his grandmother enrolled him at Grant High School in North Hollywood, where he was placed in a tenth-grade class for English as a Second Language (ESL) students. Grant High School had a large Armenian community, so Edgar was able to quickly make friends and find his way around. These high-school friends soon became his family in the United States.

A few months later, Edgar decided to look for a job so he could help his grandmother with household expenses. The manager of their apartment building was also Armenian and wanted to help out the family, so he offered Edgar a job at his water dispensary store down the street and paid him under the table. Though the job didn't pay much, Edgar was able to cover the cost of his bus fare to and from school and contribute to the rent and food expenses.

He also looked forward to working each day because it gave him an opportunity to interact with people and practice his English.

After three years, Edgar graduated from high school. He continued working in the water store during the day and got a second job doing electrical work with a licensed contractor at night. His grandmother was getting older, and he was now the main breadwinner for the household. This put a lot of pressure on Edgar, and he worked seven days a week, twelve hours a day, in order to pay the bills. At the same time, he planned to go back to school and continue his education, since this was the main reason he had decided to move to the United States. He enrolled at a nearby community college and started taking night classes.

In 2008 at a birthday party, a mutual friend introduced him to Ani. Edgar remembered that the first moment he looked at Ani, he knew he would spend the rest of his life with her. They fell in love and

Los Angeles's home away from home for Armenian immigrants. *Courtesy of Datev Arman.*

They **found a chapel**
that performed weddings
but were told that each of them needed to
present valid
government-issued
identification,
which Edgar did not have.

after dating for eight months, decided to get married. Although Edgar told Ani about his undocumented status, she wanted to marry Edgar no matter what. Ani also wanted to help Edgar find a way to fix his immigration status.

Even though Ani was a US citizen, they were afraid to get married in California because of Edgar's undocumented status, so they decided to get married in Nevada. They drove to Las Vegas on December 5, 2008, hoping to find someone who would perform the ceremony. They found a chapel but were told that each of them needed to present valid government-issued identification, which Edgar did not have. After much discussion, Edgar presented his community college student ID, which they ultimately accepted, and the wedding ceremony proceeded.

As they returned home, they were ready to start a new life together. They moved into a small condominium in Sherman Oaks, California. Edgar continued to work as an electrician, while Ani worked as a hairstylist in a nearby salon. Together they were able to make a living and help provide for Edgar's grandmother, who was now on her own.

Edgar and Ani had a baby boy they named David. David brought tremendous joy into their lives.

They also hired an immigration attorney to assist them in changing Edgar's immigration status. Since Ani was a US citizen, they were hoping Edgar could become a permanent resident and eventually a citizen. Their attorney filed a "motion to reopen," which allows undocumented immigrants to present new information before immigration authorities. What they didn't realize, however, is that their attorney failed to provide the information within the prescribed time period, so Edgar became vulnerable to detention and deportation.

On July 21, 2011, at 7:30 in the morning, Edgar and Ani were home when they heard the buzzer ring. Ani was getting the baby ready for day care, so Edgar went to the intercom to ask who was there. The person over the speaker replied, "LAPD." Thinking the police were there to see the couple next door who had been arguing, Edgar buzzed them into the condominium complex. A few moments later, Edgar and Ani heard a knock on their front door.

Ani opened the door and saw three men in ICE uniforms. The agents stood at the door and asked if Ani knew who Edgar Akopyan was. They told her that he had to be taken into custody because of an immigration violation. Within minutes, they put handcuffs on Edgar's wrists and dragged him out of the house. One of the

Federal detention center visitation hour. *Courtesy of James Oakfield.*

agents told Ani that they were taking him downtown. Edgar felt humiliated as his neighbors watched him being taken away. He was placed in the back seat of a black sedan and driven away.

When they arrived at the detention facility, the agents took Edgar's fingerprints, and he was placed in a cell with many other people. After a twelve-hour wait, his name was called, he was handcuffed once again, placed on a bus with about thirty other people, and transported to the Mira Loma Detention Center in Lancaster, California.

There was a lengthy check-in process at the center. Edgar was stripped naked, while the officers checked for tattoos and gang symbols. Edgar's jumpsuit was yellow, indicating that he had no criminal record, whereas orange signified a criminal record. He was held in a large room with rows of bunk beds and a few open showers on one side. The room housed about seventy people.

Each detainee was woken at 6:00 in the morning to get in line for breakfast. If one person was not in line, no one would

be served any food. The same procedure was used for lunch and dinner. They were usually served peanut butter sandwiches for breakfast, burritos or burgers for lunch, and pasta or chicken for dinner.

After each meal, they were allowed a few hours of free time. They could play sports, use the gym, visit the library, or go to the church. Many of the detainees chose to work in the cafeteria or the laundry room. Although they were not receiving any pay, they were provided clean clothes or a little extra food and were allowed to see their families for an extra hour on the weekends. All of the detainees had to be back in the room and in bed each night by 10:00.

During Edgar's detainment, Ani had to adjust to life as a single mom. They lost Edgar's source of income, so she had to work full-time in order to pay their bills. Ani no longer had money to pay for day care, so she took David everywhere she went. She explained, "I was depressed and I didn't know how things would turn out. My baby

"It's called a **detention center** but in reality, **it is worse than a prison**. In prison, you are able to see visitors, sit and talk to them, and even hold them. In this detention center, **you sit on one side of a glass window** with your visitors on the other."

would cry for 'papa' each and every day. At the same time, I had to stay positive and learn all the legal stuff to get my husband back home."

Each Saturday and Sunday morning, she would put David in his car seat, drive sixty miles out to Lancaster, California, and stand in a long line to visit Edgar for two hours. They were not allowed in the same room; they could only talk through a glass window. Edgar said, "It's called a detention center but in reality, it is worse than a prison. In prison, you are able to see visitors, sit and talk to them, and even hold them. In this detention center, you sit on one side of a glass window with your visitors on the other, and you talk via phone."

During each visit, Ani gave forty dollars in cash to the sheriff, who then would count it and turn it over to Edgar. This money was used to pay for clean clothes, phone cards, and snacks from the vending machines.

After two months in detention, Edgar was released. The government agreed to review his case again, and Edgar was granted legal status. After living in the United States for seventeen years, he was finally able to get his driver's license and legally work in the country that has been his home since he was fifteen years old.

While most children are
**able to see, touch,
and hug their parents**,
Yves and his younger brother
have only been **able to communicate**
with their parents
via Skype for the past **five years**.

the distance between two screens

Amy Lin

Yves Gomes and his younger brother sat in front of a computer, waiting for their parents' images to appear on screen. While most children are able to see, touch, and hug their parents, Yves and his younger brother have only been able to communicate with their parents via Skype for the past five years. Yves and his brother live in Maryland; their parents have lived in India since their deportation. Although Yves and his brother could see their parents on the computer screen and hear their voices, the distance between the two screens is a constant reminder of their journey and their separation.

Life has not been easy living without parents these past five years. Though the two young men have been living with their relatives, Yves has learned to survive on his own and to help support his younger brother. Since his parents' deportation, Yves graduated from high school and then from the University of Maryland at College Park in 2014, with a degree in biochemistry. He has done all of this without his parents by his side to support him, encourage him, and celebrate these milestones in his life.

Yves and his parents migrated from India to the United States in 1994. Yves was a young child at the time, so he has no recollection of India or the journey to the United States. He only knew then that his mother was from India and his father from Bangladesh. Yves's parents instilled in him the values of hard work and perseverance. Because poverty limited opportunities for

Yves and his brother Skype with their parents in India, fall 2013. *Courtesy of Yves Gomes.*

Yves protests against deportations outside the White House, summer 2013. *Courtesy of Yves Gomes.*

his parents when they were younger, they always encouraged Yves to do well in school.

Yves's parents made the difficult decision to move to the United States to pursue a better life and to reunite with family members. Yves's family first moved in with his great aunt and uncle in the Maryland suburbs. He and his family quickly adapted to the new environment. His father found work as a hotel server. He would tell Yves, "I work hard so you don't have to work hard." His mother attended college and graduate school in computer science.

Yves felt like any other American teen growing up in suburbia. He learned English from his older cousins and watched *Fresh Prince of Bel-Air* and *Full House*, iconic 1990s American sitcoms. In 1995, his baby brother was born, the family's first US citizen. Yves fondly remembers the road trips he and his family took to visit family members living in other states.

Yves's parents had petitioned for asylum upon arrival in the United States. Their pending case was always a point of discomfort and anxiety for the family. In 2006 after multiple appeals, their case was finally denied. This decision led to more setbacks for the family.

In 2008, Yves's father was pulled over in Baltimore for driving with a broken taillight. A few days later, Immigration and Customs Enforcement agents raided Yves's house. Agents immediately placed Yves's father in a detention center, where they began deportation proceedings. Yves's mother found a lawyer to help the family negotiate an extension of the removal proceedings to allow them time to sell their assets before Yves's father was deported, a privilege that came with harsh consequences. As a condition of the extension, his mother had to wear a tracking device on her ankle twenty-four hours a day. She had to recharge the device by sitting next to an electrical outlet several hours each day.

While his father was detained, the family lost their main source of income. Yves's mother struggled to provide for her family. She commuted to work from Maryland to Virginia and returned home each night to care for Yves and his brother. After six months in detention, Yves's father

Yves **graduated** from **high school** and then from the **University of Maryland** with a **degree in biochemistry,** **without his parents by his side** to support him, **encourage him,** and **celebrate** these milestones in his life.

was deported to Bangladesh. A year later, Yves's mother was deported to India, and Yves and his brother were left behind with relatives. Yves's parents struggled to reconnect and finally reunited in India.

Although Yves's parents were deported in 2009, Yves was able to stay for an additional year to finish his high-school education. ICE required that Yves leave the country immediately after receiving his diploma, but Yves delayed his voluntary departure in order to attend college. In August 2012, Yves was granted Deferred Action for Childhood Arrivals. He acquired a work permit and social security number. He continued living with his great-aunt and great-uncle but still felt the pain of not being with his parents.

In the summer of 2013, Yves was admitted to the UCLA Labor Center's Dream Summer leadership program. He interned with the Asian Pacific American Labor Alliance (APALA) in the national headquarters of the AFL-CIO in Washington, DC, across the street from the White House. As part of Yves's summer project, he helped organize the APALA national convention, which brought together dozens of Asian Pacific Islander (API) undocumented youth.

Yves felt the strength of connecting with other API undocumented youth. At the convention, he met with California Congressman Mike Honda and Hawaii Senator Mazie Hirono. Yves spoke on the convention floor about his experiences and received a standing ovation in front of five hundred Asian Pacific American union leaders from around the country. Yves continues to speak out to encourage other API and South Asian undocumented students to join the fight for immigrant rights and against deportations. His parents currently live in the Middle East.

Left: Twelve-year-old Yves and his family, Christmas 2003. Right: Yves's community college graduation, May 2012. *Both photos courtesy of Yves Gomes.*

His parents had tried for several
**years to fix their
immigration status**.
They had applied for citizenship on
three separate occasions
but were **denied** each time.

life without mom and dad

Mayra Jones

May 7, 2008, marked a turning point in the life of Adrian González and his family. During the early morning hours, Adrian was woken up by a loud pounding on the front door of their apartment in Anaheim, California. A group of people wearing black suits burst into their home, demanding to see Adrian's parents. His mother, Martha Morales, his youngest sister, Aileen, his brothers, Manuel, Rodrigo, and Rigoberto, and two other family members were all sleeping in the apartment. A female officer entered Martha's bedroom where she was dressed only in her pajamas. The officer brought Martha to the living room. She quickly put on her slippers but was not allowed to change clothes before they placed her in handcuffs. The officers woke everyone up and ordered them to show identification. The agents escorted everyone to the living room, except Aileen and Rigoberto, who remained asleep in the bedroom. At this point, the men told Adrian's family that they were from US Immigration and Customs Enforcement and that they were there to deport Adrian's parents.

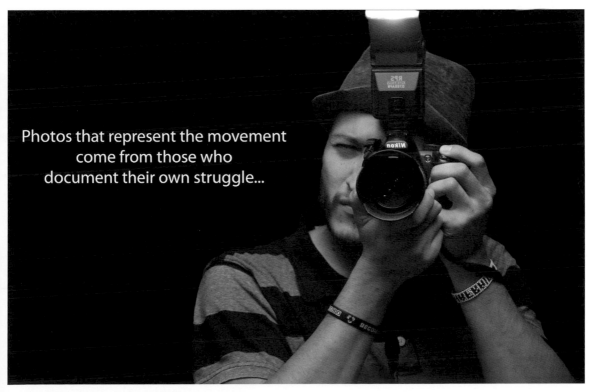

Photos that represent the movement come from those who document their own struggle...

Photographer Adrian González. *Photo by Adrian González.*

Adrian's younger brother Rodrigo, who was only thirteen at the time, witnessed his mother's arrest. Adrian couldn't believe that his own mother was being hand-cuffed before her children's eyes. Although the children were crying and panicking, Adrian's mother kept telling her family to stay calm. Adrian couldn't help thinking to himself, "Mom, you're getting arrested. How can you be so calm?" The ICE agents took her outside in handcuffs as her family watched. Finally one of the ICE agents told everyone to go back inside the house and close the door behind them. The last memory Adrian has of his mother on that early morning is of her being pushed into a van by a US immigration agent. Adrian recalls feeling a deep sense of despair; his mother was being taken away from her children, and there was nothing they could do to stop it.

Immediately after the arrest, Adrian and Manuel called their father, Juan, who was at work. They told him that their mom had been taken by ICE. Juan decided to turn himself in as well because he did not want his wife to go through the deportation proceedings by herself. That morning, he presented himself at the Santa Ana detention center in Southern California, where Martha was being held. Adrian and Manuel quickly contacted the lawyer who was helping their parents to regularize their status. However, like so many "notaries," this lawyer turned out to be a fraud and disappeared upon hearing about Martha's and Juan's detention. As the brothers tried to contact another immigration lawyer, their father called and explained that he and their mother had already been deported to Tijuana, and there was nothing further the children could do. The González family has been separated ever since.

Adrian's family is from Guadalajara, Mexico. At the age of three, Adrian came to the United States with his mother, his uncle, his five-year-old brother, Juan, and one-year-old sister, Marisol. Adrian's father had already migrated to Califor-nia a few months earlier. In Guadalajara, the González family left behind a life that

Immigrant rights activists at a civil disobedience action, San Francisco, California, October 2013. *Photo by Adrian González.*

Adrian's role in the family
changed drastically.
He now had to
take care of his
two younger brothers,
who were thirteen and eight years old.

Adrian does not remember. What he does remember is that his parents came to this country with hope for economic security and opportunities that were not available back in Guadalajara.

The González family crossed the border on foot in the 1980s when the US-Mexico border was not as highly militarized as it is today. Adrian's family divided into groups and hid in bushes to avoid detection by the US Border Patrol. Once they arrived in California, they stayed with family members in Anaheim, where they ultimately settled.

Life in the United States was not easy, but the González family was able to attain some economic and social stability through hard work. Adrian's parents were continuously employed during their time in the United States. His father worked from the day he set foot in the United States until the day he was deported. He worked as a welder in a factory, Monday through Friday and sometimes Saturday, leaving home at 5:00 in the morning each day and returning home at 6:00 in the evening. His mother was employed as a garment worker for several years. She sewed bathing suits from 9:00 to 5:00, Monday through Friday. In her last job, she washed linens and towels for hotels and restaurants.

Adrian's family was able to rent their own apartment in Anaheim. But life was

not easy. They lived across the street from Disneyland, but they only went there a few times. While the family was financially strapped at times, Adrian never went without food or clothing. The González family also opened their apartment to friends and family members when they needed shelter.

Adrian's family valued their time together and enjoyed their lives in California. On free weekends, they would attend soccer games, picnic in the park, organize family celebrations, or shop at garage sales. Adrian lived a life similar to many of his peers. He attended elementary and middle school in Anaheim. He only learned of his undocumented status when he entered high school. At the time, he couldn't fully comprehend the impact this would have on his life. He was hopeful that he would be able to resolve any issues that arose as a result of being undocumented. Adrian did not have a social security number when he applied to college and did not know that some states require it to enroll. During his senior year of high school, he realized how hard it would be to get a job or to attend college without a social security number.

When he graduated from high school in 2005, he enrolled at Santa Ana Community College. The enrollment process was new to Adrian. In addition to

Immigrant rights activists block an ICE bus carrying deportees, San Francisco, California, October 2013. *Photo by Adrian González.*

the regular admissions process, he also had to complete an affidavit to qualify for California Assembly Bill 540, which allows undocumented students to attend college without having to pay out-of-state tuition. At Santa Ana College, Adrian joined IDEAS (Improving Dreams, Equality, Access and Success), a student-run organization that supports undocumented students and advocates for increased access to higher education. IDEAS was the only student club he joined because it was for students just like him. He had no idea, however, how much support they would provide after his parents' deportation.

One day when he returned home from school, Adrian found his parents and his sister Marisol crying in the living room. His parents had received a letter from ICE ordering them to return to their country of origin. His parents had tried for several years to fix their immigration status. They had applied for citizenship on three separate occasions but were denied each time. On their last attempt, his parents

pleaded special circumstances. Adrian's brother Rodrigo had been diagnosed with a learning challenge, and he required special classes that were only available in the United States. Although they were hopeful the prosecutor would rule in their favor, the final appeal was denied.

Adrian's parents received a final letter from ICE ordering them to voluntarily leave the country within thirty days. Martha and Juan received the letter two weeks after the stamped date, which left only two weeks to seek legal advice or to prepare to leave the country. Adrian and his father immediately went to an immigration lawyer. The lawyer told Juan that his case was missing supplemental materials related to his son's special education classes and asked Marco to bring a letter from Rodrigo's school to verify his progress. The lawyer charged them about three hundred dollars for legal services, even though Juan and Martha were facing imminent deportation. Juan was desperate to fix his status, so he paid the attorney and gave him the school progress report. Juan and Martha thought that the attorney had delayed their deportation. It was not until May 7, 2008, when ICE appeared at their home, that they learned the immigration lawyer had deceived them.

Six years have passed since Adrian's parents were deported. Six years have passed since Adrian, Manuel, and Marisol have seen them. Their parents were notified that they face, at minimum, a ten-year ban to reenter the country. And even after the ban expires, there are no guarantees that their parents will be allowed to return to the United States.

Adrian's parents decided that it would be best for their children to remain in the United States to complete their education and to seek better opportunities. Adrian's parents and their youngest daughter Aileen live with friends in Tecate, Mexico, because it is closer to the US border than Guadalajara. Two of the children, Rodrigo and Rigoberto, are US citizens, so they can travel to Mexico and spend time with their parents and younger sister during school vacations. But it is difficult for Adrian's parents to get together with their youngest children who are also US citizens, because the children have to find someone to drive them three hours from Anaheim to Tecate.

Life in Mexico has not been easy for Adrian's parents. For a short period of time, Martha was working at a school supplies store. She is currently unemployed and sells homemade scarves and bracelets to help support the family. Sometimes she sells used clothes that her children send her from the United States. Juan works as a handyman and uses his welding skills for jobs here and there. But they do not have a secure income, and there are days when they cannot afford to buy food.

Adrian felt very lonely after his parents were deported. He was uncomfortable speaking to anyone about

Through activism, Adrian found balance and **emotional strength** to cope with the **separation of his family.**

Adrian photographing the Orange County Dream Team's #Not1More action, Santa Ana, California. December 2013. *Courtesy of Blu Gutierrez.*

what he was going through, and he often cried himself to sleep. At one point, he even contemplated returning to Mexico with his parents. Feeling angry and hopeless, his siblings frequently argued with one another, though they still remained close throughout the ordeal.

Adrian's role in the family changed drastically. He now had to take care of his two younger brothers, who were thirteen and eight years old. His sister Marisol had a husband and two children. His older brother, Manuel, was also married and had children of his own to support. Fortunately though, Manuel was able to provide some financial support to help pay for rent and food, which allowed Adrian to concentrate on applying for scholarships so he could continue attending community college.

In the end, Adrian decided to stay in Anaheim and continue his education at Santa Ana Community College. He realized that his younger brothers needed him, but he also became an activist to oppose the policies that resulted in the separation of families like his. Through work with IDEAS and Orange County Immigrant Youth United, he became involved with the undocumented immigrant youth movement. Through activism, Adrian found balance and emotional strength to cope with the separation of his family.

Adrian has developed skills as a photographer, and he takes pictures of the protests, marches, hunger strikes, and civil disobedience actions organized by immigrant youth throughout Southern California. He also uses his photography to capture the daily struggles of undocumented immigrants. Adrian believes that while Deferred Action for Childhood Arrivals has been a great achievement for immigrant youth, it is not enough because it excludes the majority of undocumented immigrants. He knows first-hand the impact of deportation: "ICE breaks into people's homes, tears families apart, and destroys lives. They arrest people and criminalize them for wanting a better future."

After receiving DACA, Adrian and his brother Manuel finally got their driver's licenses. They were able to drive to Friendship Park in San Diego to visit their parents through the fence along the border. For their family, it was a beautiful moment in a horrible location. But to be able to hear each other's voices and see each other again after so many years was worth it.

Adrian continues to work as an activist and photographer to stop deportations.

Abraham Medina at an immigration rally in Orange County, California, summer 2013. *Photo by Adrian González.*

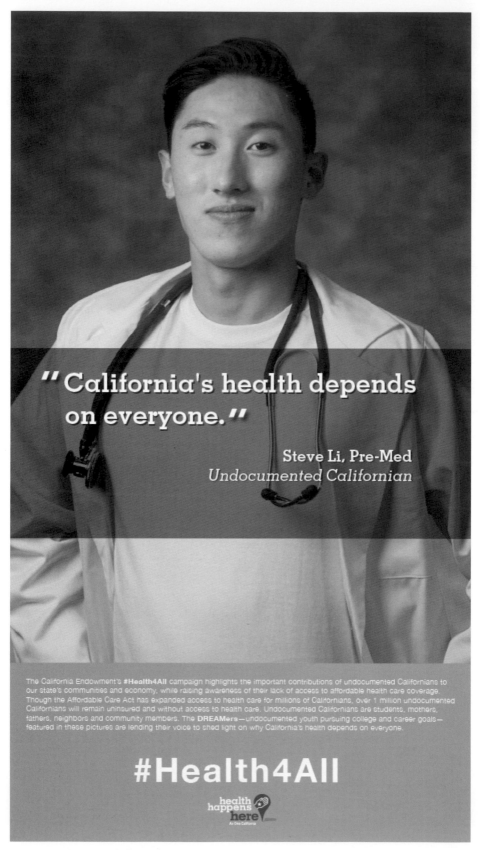

Courtesy of The California Endowment.

bring home steve li

Amy Lin and Steve Li

Steve Li was getting ready for school in the bathroom of his home in San Francisco when he heard the doorbell, followed by a heavy pounding on the door. Steve's mother was preparing for work, and she answered the door. Steve heard male voices that sounded angry, and he heard his mother's fearful voice. Steve came out of the bathroom to try to protect his mother. The men in their apartment were dressed in black, wearing uniforms with the word "ICE" printed on the back. His mother was distraught, but he had no idea what was happening or why his mother was so afraid of these men.

Moments later, Steve was hauled away from his home where he had lived for the past six years and taken to a detention facility in Sacramento. After a month in a Sacramento County jail cell, he was transferred to Florence, Arizona, where he would await his deportation to Peru.

Steve was enrolled at the City College of San Francisco (CCSF), where he was pursuing a degree in science. While he was detained, his friends, professors, mentors, and community rallied behind him with the legal help of Sin Yen Ling, senior attorney at the Asian Law Caucus in San Francisco. They formed the "Bring Home Steve Li" campaign to stop his deportation. His friends made presentations to class-rooms, reached out to community organizations for support, and contacted government agencies to advocate for Steve's release from detention. They galvanized public support through social and traditional media, including foreign media outlets, to build momentum for the campaign. With the help of the Chinese for Affirmative Action organization, Steve's supporters collected over five thousand signatures on a petition.

The "Bring Home Steve Li" campaign was one of the **most publicized deportation campaigns** to date in 2010 and the first for an **Asian American undocumented youth**.

The campaign focus was on Congress and the federal government, but they also sought support from local leaders. Resolutions to stop Steve's deportation were passed unanimously by San Francisco's Board of Supervisors, Unified School District, and City College Board of Trustees. On November 5, 2010, Steve's friends organized press events at the City College of San Francisco. Speakers included San Francisco Supervisor Eric Mar, Attorney Sin Yen Ling, Michelle Yeung from Chinese for Affirmative Action, who read his mother's statement, CCSF Professor Sang Chi, and CCSF Trustee Lawrence Wong.

The "Bring Home Steve Li" campaign was one of the most publicized deportation campaigns to date in 2010 and the first for an Asian American undocumented youth. News of the campaign appeared on the home page of Yahoo News and in the *San Francisco Chronicle*, *Sing Tao News*, *World Journal*, and various other media outlets. Steve's campaign also provided some of the background and insight for "Education Not Deportation: A Guide for Undocumented Youth in Removal Proceedings," published by the Asian Law Caucus, Educators for Fair Consideration, DreamActivist.org, and the National Immigrant Youth Alliance (2012).

Steve's parents were born in China but migrated to Peru, attempting to escape economic hardship. Steve was born in Peru and grew up speaking Spanish and Cantonese. Steve's family ran a small Chinese restaurant in Lima. Both of his parents, his sister, and Steve worked long hours every day to make ends meet. Steve watched his parents work constantly to eke out a living and grew up always wondering why they had to work so hard to survive. They experienced the extreme poverty, violence, and corruption of Peru. Conditions for Steve's family went from bad to worse when their restaurant was vandalized and their family was threatened.

In 2001, Steve's parents decided to move to New York to start a new life. Steve hoped

Steve at a civil disobedience action outside the LA Metropolitan Detention Center, summer 2013. *Courtesy of Pocho1.*

that the move would bring his family closer together. He also hoped that his parents would not have to work as hard to survive in this land of affluence and opportunity. In New York, Steve's parents found work, but the conditions were no better. They both ended up in the restaurant industry earning low wages and working even longer hours than in Peru. In 2003, the opportunity arose for the family to move to San Francisco. While Steve was sad to leave his friends in New York, he believed that the move was for the better. Maybe this time, his parents could find an easier life, and the family could spend more time together.

The dreams for his family were shattered the day ICE agents came knocking on the door. Steve's parents were deported to China, and ICE was planning to deport Steve to Peru, even though he had no family there. Thanks to the community campaign and eventual intervention of Senator Feinstein, the threat of Steve's deportation was removed, but he was told that nothing could be done for his parents. The deportation of Steve's parents proceeded without public attention because there was no immigration bill or support for undocumented parents. Steve could not fathom why he was being treated differently from his parents. He credited his parents' hard work and sacrifice for his own success. After their long and arduous journey in search of a better life, his parents were separated from their children and sent back to a country they had left decades before.

Steve has emerged as an immigrant rights activist. He joined ASPIRE (Asian Students Promoting Immigration Reform through Education) in San Francisco in 2010, the first organization in the nation led by Asian Pacific Islander undocumented youth. He participated in the UCLA Labor Center's 2011 Dream Summer internship program and worked in a community health care clinic to support the health needs of Asian immigrants. His story has been featured in the media, and his image appeared on a "#Health4All" statewide billboard campaign, promoting health care for undocumented immigrants.

After the deportation of his parents to China, Steve graduated from the University of California, Davis. He is passionate about reforming the health care system in the United States and increasing access to health care for underserved communities of color. He hopes to go on to graduate school and become a health care professional.

Left: The #Heath4All campaign in Northern California, winter 2013. Right: Steve and Carol's Montes, one of the first undocumented students to go to medical school, winter 2013. *Both photos courtesy of Steve Li.*

Reference

Asian Law Caucus et al. 2012. "Education Not Deportation: A Guide for Undocumented Youth in Removal Proceedings." http://www.e4fc.org/images/E4FC_DeportationGuide.pdf.

traffic lights

Steve Li

1, 2, 3, 4
My mind races as I look down through a window
A window that does not open
My only view into the outside world
As I look below I see bright lights puncturing through the darkness
moving around like tiny ants traveling in a line
These lights remind me of the streets that I once used to walk on
The streets of downtown San Francisco
with the bright lights of storefronts and the electrifying air full of life
and energy
But instead I'm deep inside. Here.
Trapped between four walls
Covered with gray paint with scratches and pencil marks
That decorate the walls with bible verses of hope, faith and forgiveness
5, 6, 7, 8
Books that I borrowed from my local library are due next month
My biology midterm is in two weeks
My best friend's birthday is in eight days
How long will I be here for?
I'm frozen, stuck in time
I no longer have a sense of time or space
Immobilized, paralyzed, forgotten
Like a childhood toy put away into the attic
9, 10, 11, 12
Yesterday night
11 pm I am sitting in the twenty four hour Starbucks
Flipping through pages and text of how DNA translates into RNA
Studying 'til my eyes can barely stay open
Doing what society has told me all along
to work hard and study hard
and you will be able to achieve your dreams
Today
I am
Laying still in this cold hard bed
despised by society for trying to fit into the mold that they wanted me to be
trapped behind an impenetrable door
A door without a door knob

with dents and scratches of previous prisoners who tried to escape
A door that separates the desirables from the undesirables
13, 14, 15, 16
My future no longer matters
I no longer know the realms between reality and imagination
I am tired and exhausted from the events of the last 48 hours that I
can barely comprehend
I'm just hoping to wake up from this horrible nightmare
If I could only just
close my eyes
drift off to sleep
Hoping that when I wake up
I will be back in my room with a small wooden desk, a laptop and
a pile of homework from my 19 unit workload that I'm taking this
semester
That I will wake up to the aroma that seeps into my nose every
morning of the bold and familiar smell of coffee that my mother
brews every morning
That I will wake up and hear the sounds of her heels taking careful but
strong steps as she heads out to go to her twelve hour work shift
17, 18, 19, 20
Yes, 20 seconds
That's how long it takes for the traffic light
to turn from green to red
20 seconds
That seem to last a lifetime stuck in this cell
20 seconds
The only thing that I hold onto to remind me of the life outside,
While I am. Here.
Inside. Laying still.
Immobilized, paralyzed, forgotten
Never in my life have I felt so small, so weak, so helpless
what I once thought was bright and secure
is now dark and uncertain.

The two younger siblings
applied and qualified for
**Deferred Action for
Childhood Arrivals**.
No longer did they live with the **daily fear
of deportation** and for the first time,
they could legally work.

a family united by a cause

Felipa Gonzalez

When Vicky decided to come to the United States in the 1980s, there was no fortress along the border. An imaginary line in the desert separated two countries. Although no physical barrier existed, the political and psychological chasm was huge.

Vicky's decision to cross the border was motivated by love for her mother. Her family in Mexico was too poor to pay for her mother's medication, and Vicky couldn't find a job to support her parents. She decided that she would find work in the United States. Vicky's dad knew about life across the border. He had worked as a *bracero* through a guest worker program that recruited Mexican men to work in the California produce fields, so he knew firsthand about worker exploitation and abuse. He refused to let Vicky, his oldest daughter, travel to California; she was too young, and he did not want her to suffer as he had suffered.

But Vicky knew this was the only way to provide the medicine her mother needed. At the age of nineteen and without her father's permission, Vicky decided to cross the border with her aunt. Vicky had been warned that "the coyotes eat the hens," referencing the large number of women who became victims of rape by paid smugglers,

The Bravo family at a Campaign for Citizenship event, fall 2013. *Courtesy of Osvaldo Fortes.*

"I AM FASTING FOR FAMILIES... I AM FASTING FOR JUSTICE" -JESSICA, 19

Jessica Bravo, fall 2013. *Courtesy of Osvaldo Fortes.*

or *coyotes*, during the treacherous journey across the border. Vicky and her aunt were unprepared for the cold nights in the desert, they didn't have enough water for the journey and worst of all, they witnessed brutal mistreatment of their fellow travelers by the US Border Patrol. Near the border, helicopters launched tear gas to stop migrants from fleeing. On the ground, Border Patrol agents traveled on horseback. In the rush to round up migrants, the horses sometimes stomp and injure fleeing migrants. Vicky would never forget the screams and cries of the women and children who were injured in the desert.

Vicky and her aunt were lucky and were able to avoid the Border Patrol during their crossing. On their northward journey to San Diego, their last challenge was running across a busy freeway. Although Vicky was happy she made it to California, she knew her arrival was just the beginning of more challenges.

The city of Costa Mesa, in Orange County, California, became Vicky's new home. Like many who migrate to the United States, Vicky worked several jobs. She would start her mornings working at a flower shop, return home in the afternoon to clean the house and prepare food for the family she was living with, and then work in the evenings as a janitor cleaning office buildings. She scrubbed the toilets, cleaned and restocked the bathrooms, mopped the floors, and emptied the garbage bins. Her evening shift would end at four in the morning. This was her daily routine for a full year. Vicky would cry from the exhaustion. She also lived in fear of being stopped on her way to and from work by immigration agents. She had to constantly remind herself she was doing all of this for her mother.

Vicky met a young man in California named Enrique Bravo. Both of them were struggling with life in the United States, but they were able to share their stories and support one another. But before long, Vicky received tragic news from home. Vicky's younger sister passed away unexpectedly, and her family needed her. Vicky and Enrique decided to return to Mexico together.

Vicky and Enrique tried their best to reestablish lives back in Mexico. Vicky was reunited with her family and could care for her mother. Vicky and Enrique married and were blessed with three children, Luis, Daniel, and Jessica. They saved money and opened a small store. As the economy worsened, however, it became difficult for the Bravo family to maintain the store. They fell into debt and with three children to feed,

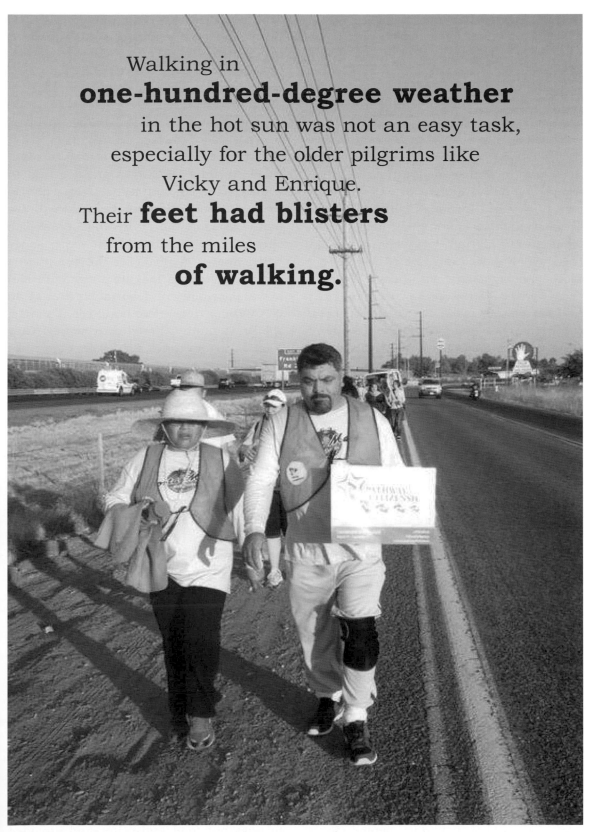

Walking in **one-hundred-degree weather** in the hot sun was not an easy task, especially for the older pilgrims like Vicky and Enrique. Their **feet had blisters** from the miles **of walking.**

Vicky and Enrique Bravo walk from Sacramento to Bakersfield to call attention to the need for immigration reform. *Courtesy of Osvaldo Fortes.*

they were barely able to survive. Enrique believed that crossing the border once again was the only way to provide for his family. Enrique made the northward trek in search of work, while Vicky stayed in Mexico to try to keep the store afloat and care for their children.

Enrique found work back in the United States but all the while, he was searching for a way to reunite his family. He met a friend who had children close in age to his own. Vicky and Enrique's children flew to Tijuana, and Enrique's friend helped them cross into California. Vicky chose to make the journey on foot and decided to bring her mother along so that Vicky could care for her. Over the course of several weeks, Vicky and her mother made multiple unsuccessful attempts to cross the border. On their third attempt, a coyote offered to drive them across the border in his car. During the trip, their car crashed, and the coyote fled the site. The Border Patrol arrived on the scene and accused Vicky of being the coyote.

In the detention center, Vicky was separated from her mother and subjected to extra abuse and bullying because they suspected that she was a coyote. During the interrogation, Vicky was thrown to the ground and kicked in the stomach by an agent. While most of the detainees were deported back to Mexico, Vicky and her mother were held for two additional days for further investigation.

After being deported, Vicky and her mother tried to obtain visas. On their third attempt, their visa request was granted, and the family was finally reunited in California.

Vicky and Enrique had a fourth child, Alex, who was born in the United States and is the only member of the family who is a US citizen. Life for the three older children was challenging. As undocumented students, their options were limited. Unlike their friends, they weren't eligible for college financial aid, they couldn't get driver's licenses, and they couldn't legally work. They hid their undocumented status for fear of deportation. In 2012, however,

their status improved dramatically. The two younger siblings applied and qualified for Deferred Action for Childhood Arrivals. No longer did they live with the daily fear of deportation and for the first time, they could legally work.

Vicky and Enrique became involved in OCCCO (Orange County Congregation Community Organization) through their church. OCCCO's purpose was to empower the community to create change. An OCCCO organizer encouraged the Bravo family to come out of the shadows and to speak in public about their experiences being undocumented. For the family, this was a big step, as they were always fearful of the possibility of deportation. But at an OCCCO meeting before hundreds of people, the Bravo family shared their stories. They went on to join the campaign for immigrant rights and met with members of Congress to share the family's stories time and again. The Bravo children participated in phone banking, attended rallies, and participated in community forums.

In the summer of 2013, in conjunction with its statewide network, OCCCO planned a one-month statewide pilgrimage on foot to push for just immigration reform. Vicky was an OCCCO leader but did not want to participate in the pilgrimage because it would require being away from her children for a whole month. She was concerned about the loss of income if she didn't work and about who would cook and care for her children, especially Alex, their youngest who was only ten years old. With the support and encouragement of the older children who promised to look after Alex, Vicky and Enrique signed up for the 285-mile pilgrimage.

In August, eleven "pilgrims" began the walk from Sacramento to Bakersfield, through the Central Valley of California. Vicky and Enrique were two of only a few undocumented participants. Their daughter Jessica came along as well. She helped to pass out food and water and provided moral support for her parents and the other pilgrims. Among the other participants were DACA recipients as well as citizens who had undocumented family members.

Walking in one-hundred-degree weather in the hot sun was not an easy task, especially for the older pilgrims like Vicky and Enrique. Their feet had blisters from the miles of walking. On the first week of the pilgrimage, Vicky did not get much sleep. The pilgrims got up at four in the morning to start their walk at five. They stopped around noon and participated in public events at churches and other religious institutions, where the pilgrims shared their stories. The pilgrims met with congressional representatives along the way, asking for a compassionate immigration reform bill that would include a pathway to citizenship.

On one very hot day, the group felt especially tired. One of the pilgrims had fainted, and Vicky was also feeling dizzy and weak. An organizer followed behind to look after the pilgrims and to photograph the pilgrimage. One of the photographs showed bare footprints along the trail. Because none of the pilgrims had taken off their shoes, they believed

that it was a message from God saying, "I am here with you, I have never left you, and you are not alone on this dangerous path." This provided the strength they needed to continue their journey. Their feelings of fatigue dissipated.

After the one-month journey, the pilgrims arrived at Fox Theater in Bakersfield and were greeted by a crowd of over two thousand people. The theater could only accommodate fifteen hundred people, so some gathered in a smaller room, and many others stayed outside to chant. Afterwards, more than two thousand people marched to the office of Congressman Kevin McCarthy, a leading Republican from Bakersfield who opposed immigration reform. The group left an altar outside of his office with items that symbolized what was left behind by people who had been deported.

Vicky and Enrique Bravo's journey to the United States began on foot, crossing the desert, searching for a better life. Their 285-mile pilgrimage was another long journey on foot, but this time they were surrounded by thousands of friends and supporters joining with them in their fight for immigration reform.

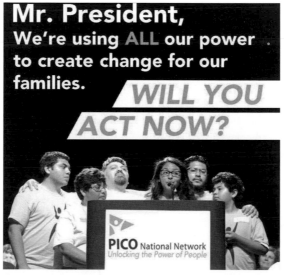

Vicky, Enrique, and Jessica Bravo at a PICO convening, fall 2013.
Courtesy of Osvaldo Fortes.

Part II

stories of resistance

The Dream 9 in Mexico. *Courtesy of NIYA/Steve Pavey.*

Illustration by Raymundo Hernandez.

In 2010, immigrant youth gained national prominence during their campaign to pass the federal DREAM Act, which would have provided a pathway to citizenship for undocumented youth who attend college or serve in the US military. By publicly declaring their status and risking arrest and deportation, immigrant youth advanced a powerful national campaign for immigrant rights, breaking through the fear that has kept undocumented immigrants silent and in the shadows. By speaking out, immigrant youth have found the power of their voices and of their stories. Although Congress failed to pass the DREAM Act in December 2010, the immigrant youth movement has continued to gain momentum.

Immigrant youth have increasingly spoken out not only to support educational access for undocumented students and passage of the DREAM Act but also to advocate for the end of the deportations that have terrorized immigrant families and communities. These campaigns have put a human face on the issue of deportation and have challenged the notion that the people being deported are criminals. Immigrant youth have blocked detention centers, stood in front of buses, and shone a spotlight on the record rates of detention and deportation under the Obama administration. These stories reflect the courage of immigrant youth who are advancing nonviolent, direct-action campaigns to challenge deportations.

"No papers,

no fear!

Immigrants are

marching here!"

Illustration by Favianna Rodriguez.

It's not an easy fight;
it takes **energy,
commitment, love**,
and it can be **absolutely terrifying**
not knowing
when we will win
or **what we will win**.

operation butterfly: reuniting with my mother

Renata Teodoro

I was six years old when my mother told me we were going to the United States to reunite with my father. My father had been working in the United States for many years, and we survived on the money he sent us. When my mother told me we were going to the United States, I remember crying and not wanting to leave my home in Brazil. But my mother said Mickey Mouse lived in the United States, and that helped ease my doubts.

My mother took the three of us, my two-year-old sister, my nine-year-old brother, and me, and we flew from Brazil to Mexico. We then took several buses to reach Tijuana. We crossed the border from Tijuana into San Diego through the desert. Some might say that my mom is a criminal because she crossed without documentation but to me, she is a hero striving for a better life for her children. When I finally saw my dad for the first time in three years, I completely forgot about Mickey Mouse. All that mattered was that we were reunited as a family again.

We first settled in Duluth, Minnesota, but after living there a year, my parents decided to move to Massachusetts to be closer to their friends. Eventually we settled in Brockton, where my parents found jobs—working at a fish factory, washing dishes, baking at Dunkin' Donuts, and cleaning houses. My parents worked tirelessly so that we would have a home, clothes, and food. After many years, they had saved enough money to open two small businesses of their own.

The Borges Teodoro family. *Courtesy of Renata Teodoro.*

Unfortunately, our family was not able to stay together. My parents tried unsuccessfully to change our immigration status. My father filed for political asylum but was denied. In 2001, he was told to leave the country. Soon after my father went back to Brazil, my older brother dropped out of high school to work full-time to help support our family.

I was a bookworm, and I poured myself into my studies. I wanted to study and work hard because my parents never got to finish high school, let alone go to college. During my senior year in high school, I was awarded a scholarship, but I wasn't able to receive it. As an undocumented student, I was not eligible for financial aid or student loans. Massachusetts also required undocumented students to pay out-of-state tuition, which was much higher than tuition for in-state residents. In spite of these barriers, I was determined to find a way to attend college. I used all the money I had saved from working while I was in high school and with additional help from my family, I entered the University of Massachusetts, Boston. I believed everything would work out and that I would be able to graduate from college as long as I worked hard and had my family's support. But I was wrong.

One day just before my second semester, while my mother and I were out at work, Immigration and Customs Enforcement came to my home and detained my older brother, searched my home to find my mom's passport, and told my fifteen-year-old sister that they would be back for the rest of us. That night I didn't sleep. The home that we worked so hard for, that I loved coming back to every day, and where we celebrated birthdays and Christmases, felt more like a prison. I didn't understand why my family was being separated, and I was angry. I was angry that my brother was

being held in a detention center after living in this country since he was nine years old. I was angry that my mom was depressed. I was angry that my sister stopped going to school because she was afraid.

I decided that no matter what happened, I was going to stay in the United States. Unfortunately, my mother and brother did not have the option to stay. With the deadlines ICE gave them, the threat of ankle bracelet monitors and random home visits, they chose voluntary deportation rather than delaying the process further through appeal.

After my family was deported, I was lucky to find the Student Immigrant Movement (SIM). SIM was the first organization I had ever heard of with undocumented students leading campaigns themselves and not just following others. I was hooked. I met students who were also undocumented and organizing for their rights. I pushed out of my comfort zone and for the first time in my life, told my story publicly to strangers. Coming out as undocumented was extremely scary. At the time, there weren't many undocumented youth willing to disclose their status. After coming out in several media articles under my real

Renata at the University of Massachusetts, Boston, fall 2011. *Courtesy of Elias Polcheria.*

Renata with other SIM leaders at the United We Dream Congress, 2014. *Courtesy of Renata Teodoro.*

name, I got text messages calling me an "illegal alien freak" or telling me to "go back to Mexico."

Although there were risks involved in coming out as undocumented, I also felt free—free from this secret I had been keeping since I was six years old. I loved being a part of SIM, and I spent all of my free time working with them. Eventually I quit my two jobs to focus on fund-raising for SIM so that we could build a strong organization run by undocumented young people.

On April 19, 2013, the day of the Boston marathon bombing, I was at home because the entire city of Boston had been told to stay inside while police searched for the bomber. I remember feeling absolutely lost. I couldn't understand the senseless violence, and I struggled with the thought that this was only a fraction of what people experience in other parts of the world. At that moment, I just wanted to be with my mom. I wanted to hold her tight, tell her I loved her, and tell her how much she was still part of my life even though she was not physically with me. There and then, I told myself I was going to make it happen no matter what; I would see my mother.

That same day, I received a call from Michele Rudy, an organizer with United We Dream, the national network of undocumented immigrant youth. Michele told me about the idea for an action that we named Operation Butterfly. The name was inspired by the artwork of Favianna Rodriguez, who drew images of butterflies as a metaphor for migration. We were talking about how beautiful that image was and how we wanted to be like butterflies so that we could move freely to be with our families without worrying about borders.

Michele asked me if I would be willing to reunite with my mother at the border, and I automatically said yes. Reflecting back, I didn't think through what that would mean. All I wanted was to see my mom. I wasn't thinking about the risk of being so close to the border or the checkpoints to get there, even though I did not yet have DACA. I just wanted to be physically near my mom and be able to hold her. My mother also did not hesitate to take the opportunity to meet with me at the border, even though she had to take a four-hour bus ride to the closest airport, then three flights, and another two-hour bus ride, to get there. The trip took almost two full days.

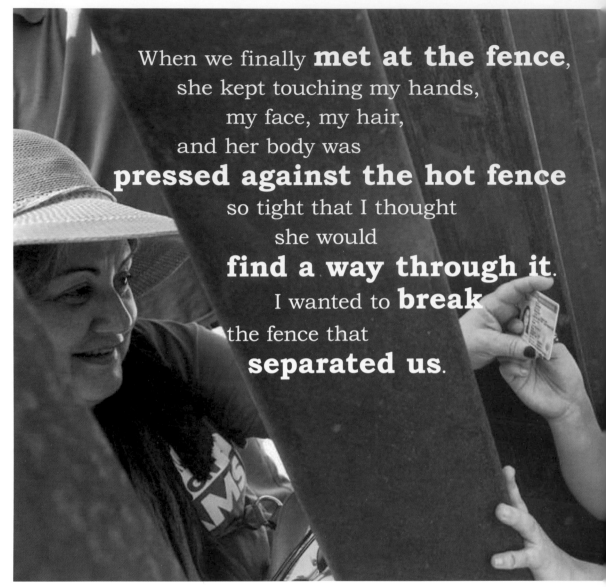

When we finally **met at the fence**, she kept touching my hands, my face, my hair, and her body was **pressed against the hot fence** so tight that I thought she would **find a way through it**. I wanted to **break** the fence that **separated us**.

Renata with her mother at the US-Mexico border, June 2013. *Courtesy of Renata Teodoro.*

Three other immigrant youth leaders agreed to participate in the action: Carlos Padilla, Evelyn Rivera, and Antonio Alarcon. They too had been separated from their mothers due to immigration laws. The next several weeks flew by. Before I knew it, it was June, and we were flying to Arizona to reunite with our moms. That day was hard on all of us because we were starting to understand how difficult our reunification was going to be. That became even clearer when we found out Antonio's mom wasn't going to be there; she had suffered an anxiety attack and couldn't bring herself to get on the flight. I remember being extremely anxious. The United We Dream team had scheduled media interviews near the border that took a long time, and I was getting frustrated. I just wanted to see my mom. Knowing that she was just a mile away on the other side of the border made me restless, eager, heartbroken, and extremely happy all at once.

After five years of working tirelessly in the Dream movement, six years of not being able to see my family, and almost twenty years since coming to the United States, I finally got the chance to see my mother

When we finally met at the fence, she kept touching my hands, my face, my hair, and her body was pressed against the hot fence so tight that I thought she would find a way through it. I wanted to break the fence that separated us. More than anything, I wanted to find a way to hug her. But I couldn't, and I felt small.

The rest of our time with our mothers went from tears to laughter. We found a way to navigate through all the years of pain and soon, we were laughing; laughing at how crazy we looked in the one-hundred-degree weather with our puffy eyes. We took selfies, exchanged gifts, and met each other's mothers. We introduced our moms to the organizers and Arizona immigrant leaders. It didn't take long before our mothers became motherly, wanting to take care of us. They wanted to buy ice cream for everyone so we weren't hot and hungry. I laughed hysterically as my mother tried to order in Spanish and how she just sounded way too Brazilian for the Mexican *paletero*, the ice cream vendor, to understand. I think those were my favorite moments and when we left, I knew we would see each other again. I couldn't wait to have more amazing moments with my mom and my family.

I am very fortunate to have been part of such a tremendous and powerful action. However, those few moments do not begin to repair the damage that immigration laws have done to my family and to others all over the country. I hope that this action is a reminder of the pain that our community is going through every single day. I hope people use this story as motivation to join this beautiful movement, even with all the uncertainties that we face. It's not an easy fight; it takes energy, commitment, love, and it can be absolutely terrifying not knowing when we will win or what we will win. I know for certain that we need others to fight by our sides for the dignity and respect our families, our communities, and all the people we love deserve.

again. When we got to the border, we first drove past our mothers, and I felt like my heart was about to explode. All of a sudden, I started panicking. I felt like I couldn't do it. I saw this huge eighteen-foot rusted fence in front of my mom, and my legs were shaking. I started to question what I was doing there. I saw my mom, and I heard her voice shaking and crying, calling me to come over: "Renata! Renata!" I felt hurt and confused. The feelings that I have been trying to put aside for the past six years came out all at once, and I could tell from her voice that she was in pain too.

When **Obama** began talking about
the upcoming Thanksgiving holiday,
Ju thought about his own family
and the
fear of deportation they face
every day.
Ju felt compelled to speak up.

i need your help, mr. president

Anayeli Y. Rivas and Amy Yu-Hui Lin

Ju Hong, an undocumented graduate of the University of California, Berkeley, interrupted the president of the United States during his speech in San Francisco on November 25, 2013. President Obama had gone to Chinatown to talk about the importance of comprehensive immigration reform. The exchange between Obama and Hong created a media firestorm and focused national attention on deportations. Ju Hong's questioning of Obama's claim that he had no power to stop deportations opened up the debate on what Obama could or should do to stop the record number of deportations under his administration.

Ironically, because of Ju's role as an immigrant student leader, he had been invited by the White House to attend Obama's speech.

As an undergraduate, Ju was student body president at Laney College in Oakland, and later, a student senator at the University of California, Berkeley. He received his master's degree in public policy from California State University, San Francisco. Ju was also a leader of ASPIRE (Asian Students Promoting Immigration Reform through Education) and a participant in the UCLA Labor Center's 2011 Dream Summer internship program. That same summer, Ju became the first Asian undocumented

Ju confronts President Obama at a press conference, November 2013. *Courtesy of* The Daily Californian.

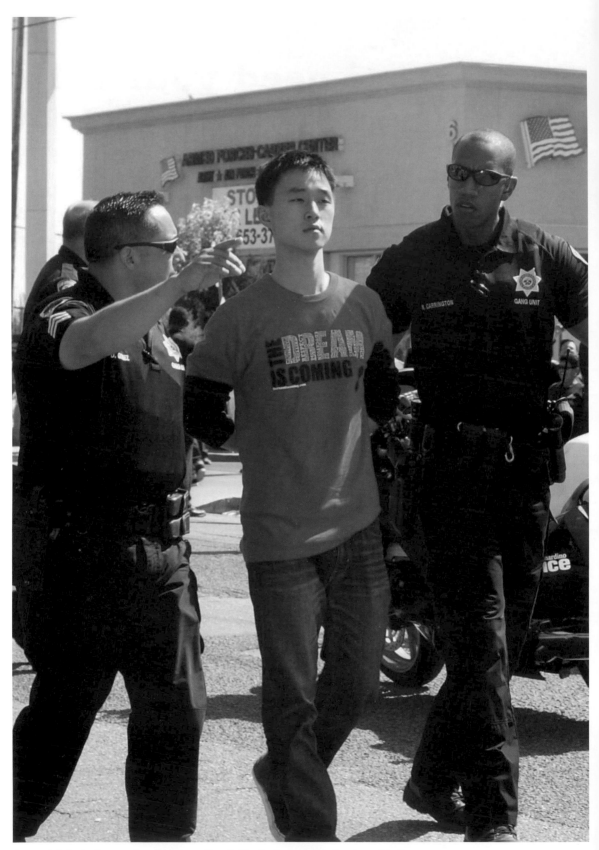

Ju at a civil disobedience action, San Bernardino, California, August 2011. *Courtesy of Ju Hong.*

That same summer,
Ju became the first Asian undocumented student to be arrested in a civil disobedience action to protest immigration policies.

student to be arrested in a civil disobedience action to protest immigration policies. He was arrested a second time to protest the appointment of Janet Napolitano as president of the University of California. Napolitano, former director of the US Department of Homeland Security, had developed and implemented policies that resulted in a record number of deportations under the Obama administration.

On the day before the president's speech, a group of ASPIRE members met to discuss their invitation to the presidential address. They decided to attend the speech to hear what Obama had to say, but they were uncertain what action they should take. They left the meeting without a clear plan. On the day of the speech, the event organizers approached a group of Asian students and asked if they would like to sit right behind the president. The organizers wanted to showcase a group of multiracial immigrants. Little did they know that these were all ASPIRE members, including Ju Hong.

President Obama's speech repeated many of the themes he had been addressing for years. He supported the need for immigration reform and blamed Congress for their inaction on the issue. He spoke of the need to grow the economy, to make our country more secure, and to strengthen our families.

When Obama began talking about the upcoming Thanksgiving holiday, Ju thought about his own family and the fear of deportation they face every day. He thought about his grandmother, who was sick in a hospital in Korea, and how his family could not be with her. He thought about his grandfather's death in Korea and how his family was not able to say a proper farewell. Ju also thought of all the families who have been torn apart under Obama's administration.

Ju felt compelled to speak up. He interrupted President Obama's speech and shouted, "I need your help, Mr. President. Our families are separated on Thanksgiving. There are thousands of people, undocumented immigrants, families that are being torn apart every single day. Please use your executive order to halt the deportations for all 11.5 million undocumented

The coverage **fueled a national debate** on deportations and whether **the president** can and should use **executive power to stop them**. The president's **claim that he has no authority** to stop deportations was **obviously untrue**.

Ju at a civil disobedience action against ICE in San Bernardino, California, August 2011. *Courtesy of Ju Hong.*

immigrants right now! We agree that we need to pass comprehensive immigration reform. At the same time, you have the power to stop deportations for all." Obama turned around to face Ju Hong, and responded, "Actually I don't, and that's why we are here." Other ASPIRE members chanted, "Stop deportations! Stop deportations!" Security approached the students and threatened to remove them, but Obama intervened. He said, "Don't worry about it, guys. You can stay there. I respect the passion of these young people because they feel deeply about the concerns for their families. If in fact I could solve all these problems without passing laws in Congress, then I would do so" (Hong 2013).

Following the exchange with the president, Ju was featured on several national television shows. He was interviewed in major newspapers across the country. The coverage fueled a national debate on deportations and whether the president can and should use executive power to stop them.

The president's claim that he has no authority to stop deportations was obviously untrue. It was the same position he took in 2012 when he claimed he had no authority to stop deportations of immigrant youth. In response, immigrant youth organized a campaign to send a letter signed by one hundred law professors across the nation, documenting that President Obama did indeed have the legal authority to stop such deportations. In addition, immigrant youth organized a series of civil disobedience actions nationwide, including sit-ins at Obama campaign headquarters, demanding an end to deportations. This campaign forced the president's hand and resulted in the implementation on June 15, 2012, of Deferred Action for Childhood Arrivals.

Ju Hong spoke truth to power. He sparked a national debate on the Obama administration's deportation policies and challenged the president's claim that he had no authority to stop deportations.

Reference

Hong, Ju. 2013. "President Obama, Stop Separating and Deporting Our Families." *The Blog, The Huffington Post*. December 2. http://www.huffingtonpost.com/ju-hong/president-obama-stop-sepa_b_4371244.html.

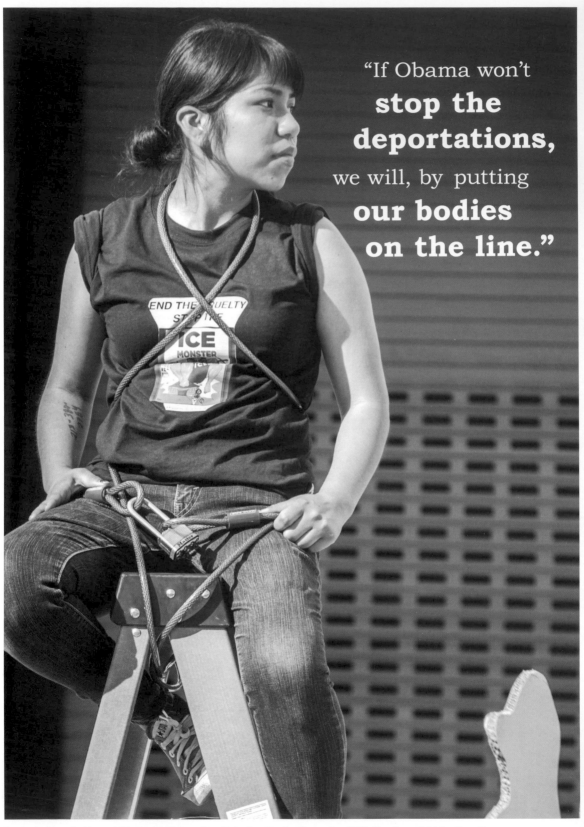

"If Obama won't **stop the deportations,** we will, by putting **our bodies on the line.**"

Ilse locked to a ladder outside the LA Metropolitan Detention Center, December 2013. *Courtesy of Adrian González.*

civil disobedience at detention centers

Maria Duque and Yadira Hernández

On the morning of December 16, 2013, undocumented UCLA graduate Ilse Escobar and four other activists from the California Immigrant Youth Justice Alliance (CIYJA) shut down the federal Metropolitan Detention Center in downtown Los Angeles. They staged a civil disobedience action and blocked the entrance and exit to the facility.

For a number of years, the detention center has been operated by the Federal Bureau of Prisons to house inmates awaiting deportation proceedings. In recent years, thousands of undocumented immigrants have been detained at this facility. The Obama administration claims that the Department of Homeland Security has prioritized deportation of immigrants with criminal records. However, many who end up in the downtown Los Angeles detention center are detained following routine traffic stops, checkpoint stops, or immigration sweeps, and then placed in deportation proceedings, even though they have no prior criminal records.

Immigrant youth organizations such as CIYJA have stepped up civil disobedience actions to draw attention to the record number of deportations that have occurred under the Obama administration. CIYJA has denounced these detentions and deportations, which have separated parents from their children and caused widespread fear and pain within immigrant communities.

Ilse Escobar came to the United States from Mexico at the age of three with her parents. She excelled in school and was admitted to the University of California,

Los Angeles, where she became a leader of the undocumented immigrant student organization IDEAS. She helped organize the Immigrant Youth Empowerment Conference, attended each year by more than a thousand undocumented students from throughout Southern California, the largest conference of its kind in the country.

Ilse has experienced firsthand the suffering caused by the separation of immigrant families. When Ilse's grandmother was on her deathbed in Mexico, Ilse's undocumented father was unable to visit his mother before her passing, as he could not risk never being allowed to return to be with his daughter. A close friend of Ilse's also experienced the trauma of having her mother detained while facing deportation proceedings.

CIYJA mobilized a hundred demonstrators to rally outside the detention center early in the morning of December 16, 2013. The protest centered around four demands of President Obama. The first was to place a moratorium on all deportations. The second was to end the federal program Secure Communities, which requires local law enforcement to turn over individuals suspected of being undocumented to immigration officials. The third demand was to strengthen implementation of the TRUST Act, a program that bars collaboration between local police and ICE. And the fourth was to demand that President Obama grant administrative relief for all undocumented people, as he had for a select group in 2012 with Deferred Action for Childhood Arrivals.

Seth Ronquillo and Ilse Escobar at a civil disobedience action outside the LA Metropolitan Detention Center, December 2013. *Courtesy of Adrian Gonzalez.*

The protestors assembled outside of the Metropolitan Detention Center and placed two ladders across the entrance. Ilse, along with Jorge Cabrera, Zacil Pech, and Seth Ronquillo, shackled themselves to the ladders with metal locks and chains around their bodies. Chloe Osmer, a fifth demonstrator, sat down between the two ladders, forming a human barricade.

During the action, community members surrounded them, holding up banners exposing the Obama administration's immigration policies and demanding an end to deportations. The demonstrators chanted, "Not one more!" and "Undocumented and unafraid, undocumented and unashamed!"

The National Day Laborer Organizing Network (NDLON) band, Los Jornaleros del Norte, played lively songs of protest.

NDLON was joined by organizations such as the California Immigrant Youth Justice Alliance, Dream Team Los Angeles, the Orange County Dream Team, and IDEAS from UCLA. When the Los Angeles Police Department officers arrived, the five demonstrators braced themselves for arrest. It was an arduous task for the officers to cut the chains and locks, remove the ladders, and arrest the five demonstrators. They were booked and released hours later. For the ten months thereafter, the five participants were in and out of court, fighting the charges. In September 2014, they pled guilty to a misdemeanor charge and paid a fine.

Edna Monroy, CIYJA Southern California regional organizer, spoke at the rally: "If Obama won't stop the deportations, we will, by putting our bodies on the line."

Members of CIYJA, DTLA, IDEAS at UCLA, OCDT, and community members stage a civil disobedience action outside the LA Metropolitan Detention Center, December 2013. *Courtesy of Adrian González.*

This was the **first time in history** that immigrant youth had **voluntarily self-deported** and were **allowed reentry** into the United States.

The Dream 9 on their way to the US-Mexico border, August 2013. *Courtesy of NIYA/Steve Pavey.*

the dream 9: immigrant youth challenge the u.s. government and win

Zara Khachatryan

Luis Gustavo León López is an undocumented immigrant student and a member of the National Immigrant Youth Alliance (NIYA.) He is one of the Dream 9, a group of undocumented students who led a national campaign to return to the United States after either being deported or leaving the country voluntarily. For the first time in history, undocumented students fought for and won the right to return to the United States.

Luis was born in Veracruz, Mexico, in 1993. When Luis was five years old, he and his family came to the United States to be reunited with his father. His father had come to the United States several years before to work and with the hope of finding a better future for his family. Over the years, Luis's father worked in many low-wage jobs so that he could send money back to Mexico to support his wife and sons.

Luis remembers seeing his father for only three short visits during the first five years of his life. Reuniting their family was his parents' top priority. Living a life in poverty in Mexico was arduous, and the future for Luis and his siblings was bleak. The government school in Luis's hometown was very poor and could not provide a quality education. In search of a better life, Luis's parents made the difficult decision to move the family to the United States.

Luis remembers the northward journey very clearly. He said goodbye to his grandmother and extended family. Luis, his mother, and younger brother took a bus from Veracruz to Mexico City where they boarded a plane to Hermosillo, Sonora, and then took a taxi to the border. They entered the United States by crossing on foot through the desert in Nogales from Sonora to Arizona. Luis's family was aided by a *coyote*, someone who is paid to assist people during the dangerous trek across the border. Luis recalls running between bushes, climbing up and down hills, crawling on his stomach, and "playing hide-and-seek" when a helicopter flew overhead. They walked all night and eventually made it to an empty lot where they slept for a few hours behind a trash container. He remembers waking up to the sound of his father's voice and running to a car for safety.

Luis's parents chose to settle in North Carolina, as his father had family who had settled there, and he could find jobs in the area. They moved into an apartment with his aunt's family, so there were eight people sharing a one-bedroom apartment. Both of his parents quickly found work.

Luis was the older of the two children, so it was his responsibility to take care of his younger brother while his parents were away. He would come home from school, clean the house, and wash the dishes so when his mother got home, she could prepare dinner. Luis adjusted to life in the United States, he learned English, and did well in school. One day, he got into a fight at school and was warned by his mother that because he was undocumented, he had to be extra careful and work extra hard in order to be successful.

Luis's mother did not speak English. Both of his parents worked long hours and did not have a network of friends for support. They had difficulty finding their way in their new environment and had limited access to information and resources. It was clear to Luis from a very young age that his life was not going to be easy. He would have to learn how to maneuver through the system all by himself.

Luis graduated from high school in 2011 and wanted to go to college, but North Carolina did not have in-state tuition for undocumented students. He was also barred from applying for most scholarships because of his undocumented status. The few scholarships that were available to undocumented students were highly competitive. After much thought, Luis decided that the only way he would be able to attend college would be to return to Mexico. Since he was the one who took care of his little brothers, he felt especially torn: "It was one of the hardest days of my life. I knew that there was no turning back as soon as I stepped onto that plane." He knew that it would probably be years before he would be able to see his family again.

Luis moved to Quintana Roo and lived with his grandmother. He tried to keep contact with his family in North Carolina, but it was hard. After every phone call or Skype session, either Luis or someone in his family would break down and cry.

Luis enrolled in a private school called Universidad Interamericana para el Desarrollo. He experienced difficulties in his classes because he was not a fluent Spanish speaker: "It wasn't easy at first. They didn't like the fact that I was raised in the United States and that I couldn't read, speak, or write Spanish well. They would make fun of my errors and would call me names like *pocho* and *gringo*." He took classes in accounting and business administration, since they mainly involved work with numbers and did not require

much reading in Spanish. It took him over a year to adjust to life in Mexico, to feel comfortable with his surroundings, and to make new friends. In June 2012, after Luis had finished his first year of college in Mexico, his mother told him that Deferred Action for Childhood Arrivals had been enacted: "It was a horrible feeling of anger, regret, and sadness all mixed together, since that was the opportunity I had been waiting for all my life and now that I had left the US, it was unavailable. I knew right then and there that I wanted to come back." Luis decided to return to the United States. He hoped that if he successfully returned, immigration officials would never find out that he had been out of the country, and he could qualify for DACA.

Luis remembered the process of crossing through the desert when he was five years old. Now as a young man, he was retracing those steps. Once again, Luis ran between bushes, climbed up and down hills, and crawled on his stomach to hide from nearby Border Patrol. This time, however, it was much more difficult to hide. Not only was he much larger but the border was also more fortified. He was caught by the Border Patrol, placed in a van, and sent to a processing center for people trying to cross into the United States.

Processing centers are even worse than the detention centers. Immigrants call the processing centers *hieleras*, refrigerators, because the officers have the air conditioning on full blast in the cells. They also never turn off the glaring lights, so people lose track of whether it is day or night. Luis said, "They would take away our sweaters and warm clothing. I didn't stop shivering for the first twenty-four hours. The only way to keep warm was to huddle in groups." They were fed bologna sandwiches on white bread three times a day. After five days, he was deported back to Mexico.

But Luis was persistent. He desperately wanted to go back to his family. So he tried again to cross—and again and again.

#BringThemHome

"Maybe this campaign was the reason I could **not cross illegally**. My return to the US was not meant to happen that way. I was intended to **cross the right way**, the way I had **dreamed of all my life**."

Dream 9 participant Luis Leon, August 2013. *Courtesy of NIYA/Steve Pavey.*

He was picked up, detained, and deported on four separate occasions. He spent many days in the hieleras from September to November of 2012. The fourth time he was picked up by immigration officers, he received a 20-year deportation order and was threatened with 180 days in jail if he tried to cross again.

Luis lost all hope of coming back to the United States and of reuniting with his parents and family. He was devastated. He decided to go back to Mexico to find a job. He thought working would distract his mind and ease the pain of being away from family.

Because of his English fluency, Luis found work as a customer service representative for a resort hotel in the Yucatán Peninsula, near Cancún. After three months on the job, he received a Facebook message from an old high-school friend. Santiago introduced him to the National Immigrant Youth Alliance and told him about a bold new campaign in the planning called "Bring Them Home." He asked Luis if he wanted to be part of a group who were planning on crossing the US border through the formal port of entry, openly challenging the US government's policies on detention and deportation of immigrant youth.

Three members of NIYA were planning to voluntarily leave the United States to travel to Mexico and risk the possibility of never being able to return. They would meet up with other youth already in Mexico, like Luis, who had either been deported or voluntarily left but wanted to return. Luis was warned, "We don't know if this is going to work. You might be locked up for six months." But Luis was willing to risk everything to return to the United States to see his family. He had about a month to prepare for the crossing. He collected all the paperwork he needed to prove that he had lived and graduated from high school in the United States. He was both excited and anxious to embark on this journey: "Something in me told me that this was the opportunity that I had been waiting for, that soon I was going to be with my family. While the possibility of getting locked up was always in the back of my head, I was very happy to be part of the group."

Dream 9 participants Luis Leon, Maria Peniche, Adriana Diaz, Ceferino Santiago, Marco Saavedra, Lizbeth Mateo, and Claudia Amaro, August 2013. *Courtesy of NIYA/Steve Pavey.*

If anyone
spoke out against the
inhumane conditions,
they were sent to
solitary
confinement.

Luis was told to meet at the Nogales-Mariposa Arizona Port of Entry on July 19, 2013, to rendezvous with the group. The crossing was to take place on July 22. Luis remembers preparing to voluntarily turn himself over to immigration officials and to be incarcerated. He recalls thinking, "Maybe this campaign was the reason I could not cross illegally. My return to the US was not meant to happen that way. I was intended to cross the right way, the way I had dreamed of all my life."

On the day of the crossing, he was filled with many emotions. He did not know what was in store. A press release to local newspapers in Mexico had generated media attention and was trending in Mexico. The action received media attention from news outlets in the United States as well. The Dream 9, as they proclaimed themselves, put on different colored caps and gowns, a symbol used by the Dream Act movement to draw attention to the US government's criminalization of young immigrants who are desperately trying to get an education. The nine young people gathered together

at the border, surrounded by a large contingent of media, and were interviewed and photographed. They created a huge scene at the Port of Entry and generated widespread media coverage on both sides of the border.

As soon as the action ended, however, they were handcuffed and sent to the notorious Eloy Detention Center in Arizona, known for its inhumane conditions. Luis described the center: "Being at Eloy was like being in a prison. They control every aspect of your life while you are there. The cells are in horrible condition. There is absolutely no privacy, and the guards treat you like criminals." Luis heard stories from other detainees who were waiting for their deportation procedures. If anyone spoke out against the inhumane conditions, they were sent to solitary confinement. Luis heard of detainees who committed suicide because of the deplorable conditions.

Luis will never forget the treatment he received at Eloy during the two weeks he was detained. He wore a green jumpsuit, which meant that he was a "level one" inmate with no criminal record. His cell was so small and narrow that he could barely move around. The showers in the corner of the pod provided no privacy. Every day they were fed the same thing, and the food was barely edible. The water was flavored with lemon but tasted like bleach. Every morning, breakfast was served at 4:20 a.m. Then there was free time in the common pod area, yard time around midday, lunch, and then they were returned to the cells for a recount. After dinner, they were again returned to their cells for a recount. The days ended at 9:30 p.m., when the guards would lock them up for the night. Luis said, "Every day I met men who had been incarcerated for very long periods of time. They were kept away from their loved ones with very little hope of getting out. Since they were trapped in a horrible prison, it seemed as if their only option was to sign the voluntary departure notice."

Members of the Dream 9 began organizing from inside the detention facility. Although the administration claimed that those in detention were criminals, in reality, most were hardworking immigrants who had been randomly picked up. Some had cases that would qualify them for release. The Dream 9 gathered stories from other detainees and reached out to their networks of immigrant rights activists to mobilize campaigns to demand their release.

When the detention officers realized what was happening, they moved members of the Dream 9 into solitary confinement. At that point, the Dream 9 waged a hunger strike to protest their unfair treatment. Dream 9 supporters generated daily media releases to expose the conditions in Eloy Detention Center. Through the hard work of the NIYA network, over forty members of

Congress signed a petition calling for the release of the Dream 9.

After two weeks of detention, the Dream 9 were released. This was the first time in history that immigrant youth had voluntarily self-deported and were allowed reentry into the United States. When he was called from his cell, Luis couldn't believe that he was being released. After two years, he could finally be with his family. The reunification with his family was the happiest moment in his life.

Luis's experience with the Dream 9 changed his life forever: "This experience helped me see who I really am and now, I have a story to tell." He returned to North Carolina and continues his involvement with NIYA. He has traveled throughout the country to share his story and to inspire other undocumented youth to take action. He helped NIYA organize the "Bring Them Home - Round Two" campaign, which sent a larger group of thirty-four immigrant youth activists through the Port of Entry in Texas. The activists were sent to the El Paso Detention Center and though some were returned to Mexico, some were released.

Luis continues to fight his political asylum case and is required to attend immigration court hearings. His future, and that of other undocumented immigrant youth, is still precarious. He plans to go back to college in the United States and will continue the fight for immigration reform that will help his parents and many other families who continue to live in fear: "It is not just about me; my family is still undocumented and at risk every day. I will continue to fight until I can be at peace, knowing that our country does not deport people in unjust ways."

Hareth understood **how desperate her parents were** to reunite with their daughters. Her parents even considered **crossing the border**, but they knew the risks involved and how many people **have died in the desert**.

wake me up: the story of hareth andrade

Felipa Gonzalez and Ludimila Alves

In the summer of 2001, eight-year-old Hareth Andrade and her two-year-old sister came to the United States from Bolivia, accompanied by their grandparents. They came to stay with her aunt, who lived in Miami. Hareth immediately realized how different life in the United States was from Bolivia. She was used to a simple life in their little Bolivian village in the Andes Mountains. That town had no paved roads, and her family lived in a small shack with limited electricity. The only thing Hareth knew about the United States was Disneyland. When she arrived in Miami, her senses were overwhelmed by the palm trees, superhighways, humid weather, and McDonald's, a place reserved for rich kids in Bolivia. She was excited to sleep in a big American house and travel in her aunt's Ford Expedition, something she had only seen in movies. Young Hareth knew that life would never be the same.

Hareth and her sister remained in the United States after their tourist visas expired, living with their grandparents. Her parents had applied for visas and were scheduled to receive them in September of 2001. However, after the terrorist attack of September 11, the US immigration system was in upheaval, and her parents' visa request was denied. They hired immigration lawyers, but to no avail. Hareth missed her parents but more than that, she was afraid she would never see them again.

Hareth Andrade in the "Wake me Up" video. *Courtesy of Alex Rivera and Aloe Blacc.*

Courtesy of Hareth Andrade.

Hareth understood how desperate her parents were to reunite with their daughters. Her parents even considered crossing the border, but they knew the risks involved and how many people have died in the desert. Hareth told her parents, "I want you here, but I don't want you dead. So you find a way to come here by plane, or don't come at all." It took three more years for her parents to finally receive their visas. Her father came first in June 2004, and on July 4, 2004, her mother came to the United States, when she was eight months pregnant. She was afraid that the airline would not allow her to board the plane, so she taped her belly and wore a big jacket to conceal her pregnancy. In the summer of 2004, the family celebrated the arrival of a new baby girl.

The transition to life in the United States was not easy for the family. While Hareth's baby sister was born a US citizen, her parents became undocumented after their tourist visas expired, limiting their job opportunities and economic security. They depended heavily on their children for their translation needs. Hareth's younger sister was in therapy to treat the trauma of growing up without her parents for so long. So although Hareth was only eleven, she assumed major responsibilities for her family.

In spite of the hardships, Hareth flourished. She did well in school and was accepted into college. At the age of seventeen, she participated in the UCLA Labor Center's Dream Summer, the first national internship program for undocumented immigrant youth. She was one of the youngest people in the program. She boarded a plane by herself for the first time and flew to Los Angeles to attend the orientation at the UCLA Downtown Labor Center. When she entered the room, she was amazed to see a hundred other undocumented immigrant students. Hareth found a community with this group of courageous young leaders.

Within the first hour, she **gathered two hundred signatures**; within the first two days, she gathered two thousand signatures; **within a week**, she reached her goal of **five thousand signatures.**

Hareth's father, Mario, at an immigration reform rally, winter 2013. *Courtesy of Hareth Andrade.*

Hareth and her father at a press conference, winter 2013. *Courtesy of Hareth Andrade.*

Her internship opportunities through the Dream Summer program included work at the national AFL-CIO in Washington, DC, where she learned about the labor movement and organizing. Hareth became an immigrant youth activist herself, and she was going to need all of those newly acquired skills and networks to address the challenges in store for her family.

One day, Hareth's father was stopped in the parking lot in front of their house for driving under the influence (DUI). Through Hareth's involvement as an immigrant youth activist, she was able to secure legal representation for her father that very weekend. Her father went to court for the DUI charge, acknowledged and apologized for his actions, paid a fine, and agreed to take DUI classes. The judge agreed to drop the charges. However, when the judge learned that her father was undocumented, he was sent to detention for deportation proceedings.

The absence of Hareth's father was very difficult for the entire family. He was no longer able to pick up his daughters from school and take them to after-school activities. But even more challenging was the fact that the family lost their main source of income. Hareth's mom doubled her work hours to support the family. The absence took an emotional toll on Hareth and her sister. Hareth had a close relationship with her father and as her twentieth birthday neared, he was gone. After waiting years for their family to be reunited, the pain of separation was present once again.

The judge and the attorney both told the family there was no legal recourse for Hareth's father to remain in the country. The news was devastating, and Hareth knew she had to take action. She wanted to go organize against her father's deportation but didn't know how. She contacted the Education Not Deportation (END) program of United We Dream, the national network of undocumented youth organizations. The director advised her to launch a petition campaign to stop her father's deportation. Within the first hour, she gathered two hundred signatures; within the first two days, she gathered two thousand signatures; within a week, she reached her goal of five thousand signatures.

Hareth was invited to represent the immigrant youth movement at the AFL-CIO national convention in September 2013 in Los Angeles. She read a poem she had written entitled "America," about the immigrant rights movement. After reading her poem, she called on the convention participants to stand up if they would help stop her father's deportation. Two thousand people rose to their feet and applauded in solidarity.

After her speech, Hareth was contacted by the staff of recording artist Aloe Blacc to see if she would appear in his music video on deportations. This offer sounded surreal to her; she couldn't believe it. She was flown to Los Angeles and learned that the video shoot was going to be at the UCLA Downtown Labor Center, in the same room where she had first participated in Dream Summer 2011. Hareth knew that this was a sign that she was in the right place doing the right thing.

In 2014, Aloe Blacc's music video "Wake Me Up" was released. The video portrays the heart-wrenching story of a family captured by ICE while crossing the border and the trauma families experience as a result of separation and deportation. The video is the story of Hareth's family, and Hareth is the featured actor. More than 6 million people across the United States and throughout the world have seen the video.

As a result of her speech at the AFL-CIO convention and the release of the Aloe Blacc video, Hareth has become one of the best known immigrant youth activists in the country. She encourages other youth to stand up and raise their voices. Hareth believes that all it takes is a little bit of interest for students to get involved. Anyone can start going to meetings, learn about the movement, work for immigration reform, and fight to stop deportations. That's how her story began. Hareth had a little bit of interest, a little bit of courage, and she began to share her story in public.

Hareth once made a promise to her grandmother to always keep their family together. She has tried her best to keep this promise. Her grandmother passed away recently, but the promise remains. After living for many years in the United States, her grandmother chose to return to Bolivia. When she became sick and was on her deathbed, no one in Hareth's family was able to visit her before she passed away; no one was able to attend her funeral. Now Hareth thinks that her work as an immigrant rights activist is part of her promise to her grandmother. Because Hareth is not just working to keep her family together—she is working to keep everyone's family together.

Hareth's father is still awaiting deportation. His case remains open to this day.

That's how her story began.
Hareth had a **little bit of interest**,
a little bit of courage,
and she began to
share her story in public.

america
Hareth Andrade

We need to talk
don't be afraid & stand
because we believe this is the year
the year that the dreams of my parents will be realized
and the dreams of millions who came and crossed borders
unimaginable, to reach the land of opportunities.
A story comes to mind
Of A little girl's dream
to become a spokesperson,
and she did not mean
To take anything
Let alone make a scene
She
Was just trying to fit in
Yet By age 15 treated like she was a sin
Illegal
Placed in a category, a shelf, a cell
Incarcerated in words
Sentenced without conviction
alone she would crumble
yet the dream kept her humble
and she built a suit of armor to join the fight.
Empowered by the liberation
we the people must build a suit
Let's go on and tell them,
While they who have the power sit
Separating us as they see fit
While my father's hands blister from work all day
and he doesn't feel like he has a say
As this nation dedicated to the proposition
that all men are created equal
Rises with 11 million dreams behind it
America, we are Liberated by the pain
So let's talk, because
America is home
A land of dreams
for all dreamers

Erika was **one of about three hundred** undocumented Arizona State University students **who lost their financial aid**. She observed that in the aftermath of **Proposition 300**, "the number of **undocumented** students enrolled at ASU dropped from three hundred **to less than five**."

erika andiola stops her mother's deportation

Blanca Alcántara

Erika Andiola was born in Durango, Mexico, where she lived with her family until the age of eleven. Erika, her young brother, and their mother, Guadalupe Arreola, left their home to escape domestic violence at the hands of Erika's father. Her two older siblings had already moved to the United States and established a life there. So like many immigrants, her family crossed the desert from Mexico to Arizona to seek a better life. She recalls, "Coming through the desert at that age, it's pretty clear that you are undocumented." Her migration odyssey through the desert

was a traumatic experience that to this day, she does not like to discuss.

Erika's family settled in Mesa, Arizona. From the moment she arrived, Erika was fearful of being deported by law enforcement. They represented the constant threat of separation from her family. She even panicked when she saw Arizona park rangers because their green and white trucks are the same colors as Border Patrol vehicles.

Erika was a good student and was admitted to Arizona State University in Phoenix. At the time, Arizona provided in-state tuition and financial aid for

Erika with her mom and brother, fall 2013. *Courtesy of Erika Andiola.*

Erika at an immigration reform rally outside Capitol Hill, fall 2013. *Courtesy of Erika Andiola.*

undocumented students who had attended public schools within the state. But this abruptly changed in 2006, when Arizona voters passed Proposition 300 (University of Arizona 2012). Undocumented college students would now not only be denied financial assistance but their tuition would also skyrocket because they no longer qualified for in-state fees. Erika was one of about three hundred undocumented Arizona State University (ASU) students who lost their financial aid. She observed that in

the aftermath of Proposition 300, "the number of undocumented students enrolled at ASU dropped from three hundred to less than five."

Erika had met many of the undocumented students at ASU. In 2009, the ASU students began organizing support for the federal DREAM Act, legislation that would grant them a path to citizenship if they attended college or served in the military. This campaign gave birth to the Arizona Dream Act Coalition (ADAC). ADAC had high hopes that the DREAM Act would pass Congress and be signed into law by President Obama in 2010. They expected that the federal DREAM Act would supersede Proposition 300. Although the House of Representatives passed the DREAM Act in December 2010, the Senate was unable to overcome a threatened filibuster by a minority of senators, and the DREAM Act failed.

That same year, Arizona Governor Jan Brewer signed into law SB 1070, the most draconian anti-immigration law in the nation (State of Arizona 2010). Opponents denounced the bill for criminalizing undocumented immigrants and promoting racial profiling. There were massive protest marches and rallies nationwide. The singer Shakira, one of Erika's idols, attended one of the mobilizations. Erika shared her immigration story with Shakira, and their conversation was picked up by the media. Erika's "coming out" story was publicized widely on television, on the radio, and in newspapers. In 2012, the US Supreme Court struck down most of the worst provisions of the bill.

Erika went on to graduate from Arizona State University. With the enactment of DACA, she was finally freed from the daily fear of deportation, and she obtained work authorization. She was hired to work in the Washington, DC, office of a US congresswoman from Arizona. Finally, she was free to apply her education and advance her career.

But the passage of SB 1070 emboldened anti-immigrant advocates like Governor Brewer and Sheriff Joe Arpaio. Arpaio was infamous for terrorizing immigrant communities with broad neighborhood sweeps, checkpoints, and workplace raids. He paraded undocumented immigrants through the streets like criminals, lining them up in orange jumpsuits and forcing them to march in the blazing desert sun. Erika explained, "Sheriff Arpaio goes to your work, confiscates your documents, looks up your address, and then goes to your house. Next thing you know, he takes you, your parents, or whoever he can into detention." The impact of the raids hit close to home when Sheriff Arpaio raided the houses of Erika's family friends and her mother's coworkers.

The **video Erika posted** created **momentum**, and thousands of people were **signing petitions** and **calling on ICE** to **stop** her **mother's deportation**.

Erika's family considered fleeing Arizona, like many other immigrants had. But her uncle was resistant and encouraged their family to stay. He was a man of faith and was hopeful that nothing would happen to them. Unfortunately, ICE raided Erika's home and took her uncle into detention. Erika and the rest of the family fled to search for another place to live because they feared ICE would return to deport them as well. The raid was a nightmare come true.

And then things got worse. In 2012, her mother was pulled over while driving in Mesa, Arizona. Arizona no longer issued licenses to undocumented immigrants, forcing them to drive without a license. Racial profiling and pulling people over for "looking undocumented" was common. Fortunately, Erika's mom was released. But four months later, ICE again showed up at Erika's house looking for her mother. They took her mother into detention along with her older brother. He was detained because he had a suspended driver's license, which was enough for ICE to assume he was undocumented.

Erika had worked on many deportation cases before and had been successful at stopping "dreamers"—a term some use to refer to undocumented immigrant youth—from being deported. ICE had issued memos deprioritizing the deportation of immigrant youth and with the passage of DACA in 2012, more immigrant youth were free from the fear of deportation. But this was the first time she encountered a deportation case of an immigrant adult. At first, she didn't know what to do. But then she realized, "What the hell am I doing? I'm an activist. I have been doing this for so long. I have been working with dreamers and other people to stop deportations, and I am here crying. This is not acceptable."

Erika went into action. She called every attorney she had ever worked with. She had just gotten a job with an Arizona congresswoman, and Erika thought, "Why am I not calling those people?" She made a video with a call to action and posted it on social media: "My mom and my brother just got detained, and we need to do something. This is real, and it can happen to anyone." She also posted on Facebook, "I will be at the processing center. Make sure that people are there so we can make a big crowd."

Erika was warned by attorneys that her mother had an expedited order of removal, which meant that she could be deported at any time without consulting an attorney or appearing before an immigration judge. Erika decided to check on her mother herself. She and one of her brothers drove to the processing center in Phoenix. When she approached one of the officers at the center, he said, "Your mom is already in Mexico. She's gone. You better stop whatever you're doing. She's gone." Erika broke down in tears and thought to herself, "That's it? I wasn't able to do anything. This is horrible." In reality, however, her mother was being held at another processing center in Florence, Arizona.

Erika continued campaigning for her mother's release. That night, she held a strategy call with attorneys and supporters to discuss how to stop her mom's deportation. When Erika went online, she saw that there were thousands of encouraging messages on Facebook and people getting involved. The video Erika posted created momentum, and thousands of people were signing petitions and calling on ICE to stop her mother's deportation.

Guadalupe, meanwhile, had been treated poorly by the officers from the moment they took her into custody. She had breast cancer, high blood pressure, and diabetes, but when she asked if she could have access to her medication, they denied her request. The agents instead kept her in the van and continued to raid other houses. After several hours, Erika's brother and Guadalupe were taken to the processing center. The agents tried to persuade her to sign a voluntary departure form, but she refused to sign any documents. Erika's brother was

Erika speaks at a rally against deportations, Arizona, fall 2013. *Courtesy of Erika Andiola.*

also repeatedly pressured to sign the form. They told him, "We are going to deport your mom. She is leaving in a few hours. You shouldn't let her go by herself." The agents also threatened him, warning him that he better not make trouble, like his sister.

Once in the processing center, the men and women were held in separate cells, so Guadalupe and her son could see each other through a glass window, but they could not talk or embrace one another.

The processing center staff took Guadalupe out of the cell around four in the morning and placed her on a bus to Mexico. On the way out, she desperately tried to find a way to communicate with her son. She noticed there was a water fountain outside her son's cell, so she told the guards she needed a drink of water. She stood by the water fountain and waved good-bye to her son. She thought she might not see him for a very long time and perhaps ever again. Erika's brother was allowed to make a call around the same time that Guadalupe was taken from the processing center. He told Erika, "I just saw them take mom out of the cell, and the ICE agent just told me she is getting deported right now."

Once on the bus, Guadalupe noticed that all the passengers were men except for her. They could not see anything through the windows, so she asked them, "Do you know where we are going? I don't know what is going on." The men told her they were getting deported and were on the way to Mexico. They explained that some of them had signed a voluntary departure while others had an expedited order of removal. Guadalupe said, "I wasn't scared at first but when they told me that we were on our way to Mexico, I got very scared." Guadalupe thought that now there was no turning back.

But then the bus abruptly turned around. The driver did not explain why they were going back. They stopped in Florence at a detention center close to the border. When Guadalupe got off the bus, she asked the agents, "Can I make a call? Can you let me know what is going on?" The officer at the detention center allowed her to call the Mexican consulate in Tucson. As soon as she told the Mexican consulate, "Mi nombre es Guadalupe Arreola," he replied, "Oh my God! You are the lady all over the news. Don't worry, you are fine now. Your daughter is doing everything she can to make sure you don't get deported. They will take you back to Phoenix in a few minutes."

When Guadalupe heard the news that she was to be released, she broke down and cried. Deep within her heart, she always knew Erika would help her: "I would have never doubted that she was going to do something." Guadalupe was granted permission to stay in the United States on a temporary basis. She was granted prosecutorial discretion, with the understanding that she would have to return for a review of her case in one year. Erika's brother had already been released, as he should not have been detained in the first place. He had been in the United States for twenty years, is married to a US citizen, and has two children who are US citizens.

Erika realized that had she not been involved in the movement, her mother would have been deported. When Guadalupe returned home, Erika vowed that she would never again feel guilty for being involved, for being an activist, and for coming out of the shadows.

When they were together safely, Erika asked her mother, "Did they hurt you?" Guadalupe described the shackles they put on her legs and the handcuffs on her wrists connected with chains. She asked the guards, "Why am I getting handcuffed? I am a fifty-five-year-old woman who has never done anything bad. How do I pose a threat to you? I won't run away. I am a sick woman." The shackles on her leg made a deep cut, and Guadalupe has a scar on her leg that will forever remind her of that horrible experience.

Even after her mother's release, Erika was afraid: "For a very long time, I was still scared that they would come back to the house. I didn't want to leave Arizona." After returning to DC for a couple of months, Erika decided to leave her position and go home to Arizona. She wanted to be with her mother to make sure she did not get deported. When Guadalupe's one-year review with ICE was approaching, Erika again started a campaign to rally community support. She was surprised when ICE contacted her directly and told her that her mother did not have to report to the ICE office. Instead, they extended her mother's prosecutorial discretion for another year. When Erika insisted on going to the ICE office anyway, she was told that the prosecutorial discretion had been extended for two years.

Erika learned a lot from the campaign to stop her mother's deportation: "I now understand that they don't see us as human beings but as numbers. They don't realize the pain that our community goes through when someone is removed from a family. They don't realize the trauma children face when an ICE agent shows up at their house and takes away their parents."

Erika's activism continues. She was recently arrested and taken to jail by Sheriff Arpaio for supporting a group of hunger strikers in Phoenix who wanted their children released from the Eloy Detention Center. The future of Erika's mom is still uncertain. But Erika will continue to fight to keep her family together and to make sure that the undocumented community in Arizona and across the country is no longer subjected to the fear of deportation.

Reference

State of Arizona. 2010. SB 1070. http://www.azleg.gov/legtext/49leg/2r/bills/sb1070s.pdf.

University of Arizona. 2012. "Proposition 300 FAQs." Office of the Registrar. https://www.registrar.arizona .edu/residency/prop300/.

Erika and her mom, fall 2013. *Courtesy of Erika Andiola.*

Courtesy of Pocho1.

resources

Get Informed

American Civil Liberties Union and Human Rights Watch. "Deportation by Default: Mental Disability, Unfair Hearings, and Indefinite Detention in the US Immigration System." July 2010. https://www.aclu.org/files/assets/usdeportation0710_0.pdf.

American Civil Liberties Union. "Know Your Rights: What to Do if You're Stopped by Police, Immigration Agents or the FBI." https://www.aclu.org/drug-law-reform -immigrants-rights-racial-justice/know-your-rights-what-do-if-you.

Asian Law Caucus et al. "Education Not Deportation: A Guide for Undocumented Youth in Removal Proceedings." 2012. http://www.e4fc.org/images/E4FC _DeportationGuide.pdf.

Capps, Randy, et al. "Paying the Price: The Impact of Immigration Raids on America's Children." A report by The Urban Institute for the National Council of La Raza. 2007. http://www.urban.org/sites/default/files/alfresco/publication-pdfs/411566-Paying-the -Price-The-Impact-of-Immigration-Raids-on-America-s-Children.PDF.

CASA of Maryland, Detention Watch Network, and National Immigration Project of the National Lawyer's Guild. "Know Your Rights! Learn How to Protect You and Your Family during Immigration Raids." http://casademaryland.org/wp-content /uploads/2014/03/KYR-booklet_English.pdf.

CASA of Maryland. "Warning: Protect Yourself from Immigration Raids!" American Friends Service Committee. July 2010. http://www.afsc.org/resource/protect-yourself -immigration-raids.

Center for Human Rights and International Justice at Boston College. "Returning to the United States after Deportation: A Guide to Assess Your Eligibility." August 2011. http://www.bc.edu/content/dam/files/centers/humanrights/pdf/Returning%20to %20the%20US%20AfterDeportation%20-%20A%20Self-Assessment%20FINAL.pdf.

Immigrant Legal Resource Center. "What Happens in Deportation Proceedings? A Guide for Immigrants in the CA Criminal Justice System." http://www.ilrc.org/files /documents/guide_on_imm_proceedings_for_crim_defendants_final_nov_2013.pdf.

Mexican American Legal Defense and Educational Fund, National Day Laborer Organizing Network, and National Hispanic Leadership Agenda. "Detention. Deportation, and Devastation: The Disproportionate Effect of Deportations on the Latino Community." May 2014. http://www.maldef.org/assets/pdf/Deportation_Brief _MALDEF-NHLA-NDLON.pdf.

National Immigration Law Center. "The All-in-One Guide to Defeating ICE Hold Requests (a.k.a. Immigration Detainers)." Available at http://www.nilc.org/pubs.html.

Get Help

#Not1More, http://www.notonemoredeportation.com

Asian Americans Advancing Justice - Los Angeles, http://www.advancingjustice-la.org

California Immigrant Youth Justice Alliance (CIYJA), http://www.ciyja.org

Central American Resource Center (CARECEN), http://www.carecen-la.org

Coalition for Humane Immigrant Rights of Los Angeles (CHIRLA), http://www.chirla.org

Detention Watch Network, http://www.detentionwatchnetwork.org

Dolores Street Community Services, http://www.dscs.org

Esperanza Immigrant Rights Project, http://www.esperanza-la.org

Families for Freedom (FFF), http://familiesforfreedom.org

Immigrant Defense Project (IDP), http://immigrantdefenseproject.org

Immigrant Youth Coalition (IYC), http://theiyc.org

Immigrant Youth Justice League (IYJL), http://www.iyjl.org

Mariposas Sin Fronteras, http://mariposassinfronteras.org

Mexican American Legal Defense and Educational Fund (MALDEF), http://www.maldef.org

National Day Laborer Organizing Center (NDLON), http://www.ndlon.org

National Immigration Law Center (NILC), http://www.nilc.org

Organized Communities Against Deportations (OCADIL), https://www.facebook.com/OCADIL

Puente Movement, http://puenteaz.org

United We Dream (UWD), http://unitedwedream.org

Know Your Rights/Conozca Sus Derechos

Many undocumented immigrants continue to live in fear of deportation and separation from their families. Here is a useful "Know Your Rights" card that can be cut out and placed in your wallet. For more extensive legal advice, consult an immigration attorney or an immigrant rights organization.

Usted tiene derechos constitucionales.

- **NO ABRA LA PUERTA** SI UN AGENTE DEL SERVICIO DE INMIGRACION ESTA TOCANDO A LA PUERTA.

- **NO CONTESTE NINGUNA PREGUNTA DEL AGENTE** DEL SERVICIO DE INMIGRACION SI EL TRATA DE HABLAR CON USTED. Usted tiene derecho a mantenerse callado.
  No tiene que dar su nombre al agente. Si está en el trabajo, pregunte al agente si está libre para salir y si el agente dice que sí, váyase. Usted tiene derecho de hablar con un abogado.

- **ENTREGUE ESTA TARJETA AL AGENTE. NO ABRA LA PUERTA.**

I do not wish to speak with you, answer your questions, or sign or hand you any documents, based on my 5th Amendment rights under the United States Constitution.

I do not give you permission to enter my home, based on my 4th Amendment rights under the United States Constitution, unless you have a warrant to enter, signed by a judge or magistrate, with my name on it, that you slide under the door.

I do not give you permission to search any of my belongings, based on my 4th Amendment rights.

I choose to exercise my constitutional rights.

Source: http://www.ilrc.org/files/documents/kyr__no_phone.pdf.